RAND | NATIONAL DEFENSE RESEARCH INSTITUTE

Fighting Shadows in the Dark

Understanding and Countering Coercion in Cyberspace

Quentin E. Hodgson, Logan Ma, Krystyna Marcinek, Karen Schwindt

Prepared for the Office of the Secretary of Defense

Approved for public release; distribution unlimited

For more information on this publication, visit www.rand.org/t/RR2961

Library of Congress Cataloging-in-Publication Data is available for this publication.
ISBN: 978-1-9774-0275-2

Published by the RAND Corporation, Santa Monica, Calif.
© Copyright 2019 RAND Corporation
RAND® is a registered trademark.

Support RAND
Make a tax-deductible charitable contribution at
www.rand.org/giving/contribute

www.rand.org

Preface

The aim of this report is to understand whether and how states use cyber operations to coerce other states or actors. It examines cases involving Russia, China, Iran, and North Korea. The report draws important distinctions between how coercion is traditionally defined in recent literature and how it may occur in reality. The report highlights the challenges of identifying cyber coercion, particularly if separated from examining the broader political and economic context. This report then proposes some pathways to developing a deeper understanding of cyber coercion and how to counter it.

This exploratory research was sponsored by the Office of the Secretary of Defense and conducted within the Cyber and Intelligence Policy Center of the RAND National Defense Research Institute, a federally funded research and development center (FFRDC) sponsored by the Office of the Secretary of Defense, the Joint Staff, the Unified Combatant Commands, the Navy, the Marine Corps, the defense agencies, and the defense Intelligence Community.

For more information on the Cyber and Intelligence Policy Center, see www.rand.org/nsrd/ndri/centers/intel or contact the director (contact information is provided on the webpage).

Contents

Summary

As the development of more connected and interconnected information systems and networks proceeds, the potential for actors to use cyber operations to exert influence and impact the economic, political, and social wellbeing of other states is growing. Cyber operations have become another tool of statecraft. In this report, we seek to understand how cyber operations can play a role in interstate relations in the space between cyber-enabled espionage and outright conflict. We ask whether states are using cyber operations to coerce others and, if so, what can be done to counter it.

Thomas Schelling described two forms of coercion: active coercion, or compellence; and passive coercion, or deterrence.[1] These two forms represent more of a continuum, as some states may combine compellence actions with the threat of more devastating consequences to accomplish their ends. One group of researchers noted that coercion is "the use of threatened force, including the limited use of actual force to back up the threat, to induce an adversary to behave in differently than it otherwise would."[2]

The scholarly literature describes a logic for the dynamic between coercer and coerced: "If you do not do X, I will do Y."[3] Another form this takes is that a coercive action or threat that "demands clarity in the expected result ... [and] be accompanied by some signal of urgency."[4] In reality, the demands of the coercer are not always so clear: The coercer may not make a clear threat or identify itself explicitly. To express this difference, we can articulate the theoretical ideal and observed practice as follows: *Coercion in theory* requires one actor to make explicit demands of another which are tied to clear consequences for noncompliance. Coercion in theory can include inflicting pain or punishment to demonstrate commitment and signal that worse is to come

---

[1] Thomas C. Schelling, *Arms and Influence*, New Haven, Conn.: Yale University Press, 1966, pp. 69–73.

[2] Quoted in David E. Johnson, Karl P. Mueller, and William H. Taft, *Conventional Coercion Across the Spectrum of Operations: The Utility of U.S. Military Forces in the Emerging Security Environment*, Santa Monica, Calif.: RAND Corporation, MR-1494-A, 2003, p. 8.

[3] Erica D. Borghard and Shawn W. Lonergan, "The Logic of Coercion in Cyberspace," *Security Studies*, Vol. 26, No. 3, 2017, pp. 452–481.

[4] Christopher Whyte, "Ending Cyber Coercion: Computer Network Attack, Exploitation and the Case of North Korea," *Comparative Strategy*, Vol. 35, No. 2, 2016.

if the threatened state or actor does not accede to the coercer's demands.[5] *In practice*, however, a coercing state may only make vague threats or even seek to covertly act to inflict some pain with the intent of motivating the coerced state to change its behavior. The specific desired behavior may not be clearly stated either. Observed practice is not always entirely ambiguous: It could involve a clear demand, but an ill-defined threat. For this report, we define *cyber coercion* as the threat (implied or explicit) or limited use of cyber operations to motivate a change in behavior by another actor that may involve cyber operations on their own or in conjunction with other coercive actions.

Case Studies

We explore case studies of potential cyber coercion for the four nation-state actors the U.S. government has identified as most concerning.[6] For each threat actor, we conducted open-source research to develop an overview of each country's cyber capabilities and published doctrine on cyber operations, and examined open-source literature on the major government-affiliated cyber operations groups. We then reviewed cyber operations that these states are alleged to have conducted against another state or actor to determine the following:

- Was there an explicit or implied threat aimed at another actor to coerce a change in behavior?
- Did the coercer make itself known to its intended victim?
- What were the broader political and economic circumstances surrounding the threatened action, and do these circumstances provide clues concerning potential coercive action?
- Were the cyber operations intended primarily to threaten or impose pain to motivate a change in behavior or for some such other purpose as espionage or retaliation?

These questions frame the case studies we examine in this report. The cases were chosen because of their potential to provide insights into competition or conflict between two states and the occurrence of cyber operations alongside other diplomatic, economic, or military activities. In addition, we reviewed two databases on cyber operations to identify potential cases and determine the scale of apparent cyber coercion as a subset of publicly known state-sponsored cyber operations.[7] Given the

---

[5] Schelling, p. 171.

[6] The White House, *National Cyber Strategy of the United States of America*, September 2018, pp. 1–2.

[7] Brandon Valeriano and Ryan C. Maness, "The Dynamics of Cyber Conflict Between Rival Antagonists, 2001–11," *Journal of Peace Research*, Vol. 51, No. 3, 2014. The Council on Foreign Relations has compiled a data set covering 2005–2018; see Council on Foreign Relations, "Cyber Operations Tracker," webpage, undated.

unclassified nature of this study, we did not have access to any private communications between the involved states or evidence of cyber activity that did not gain public attention through media coverage, official government pronouncements or reports from cybersecurity researchers.

We examine the following case studies:

- Russian targeting of Ukrainian critical infrastructure, particularly its energy grid, in 2015 and 2016
- Russian cyber operations in Montenegro as the country worked toward joining the North Atlantic Treaty Organization (NATO) and developing closer ties with the European Union
- Chinese opposition to the United States' deployment of theater missile defense systems (THAAD) to the Republic of Korea
- Iranian cyberattacks against Saudi Arabia in 2012 and 2017
- North Korean targeting of Sony Pictures Entertainment in 2014.

We found that cyber operations intended to coerce are a small subset of overall cyber operations globally. Valeriano and Maness's data set covering 2001 through 2011 only identifies four cases of cyber operations seeking to change another state's behavior, and two of those are the same operation (the joint U.S.–Israeli cyber operation against the Iranian nuclear program). The Council on Foreign Relations cyber operations tracker, which covers 2005 to the present, does not code operations by apparent intent, but by using the attack type as a proxy for intent, we see that only 23 of 288 operations resulted in data destruction or sabotage, compared with 237 cases of espionage.[8] Therefore, cyber operations are still predominantly used by states for the purpose of espionage.

Russian cyber operations appear to have had some coercive intent in Ukraine and Montenegro. In Ukraine, most notably in the attacks on the energy sector leading to power outages in December 2015 and 2016, as well as in operations impacting the media, finance, and transportation sectors in 2015, Russia sought to coerce Ukraine into drawing back from greater integration with the West and remaining in Russia's sphere of influence. Russia also opposed the Montenegrin government's efforts to join Western institutions, including NATO, calling accession talks an "additional destabilizing consequence for the system of Euro-Atlantic security" and conducting denial of service attacks against numerous government and political websites and email phishing campaigns against the government.[9]

---

[8] The other categories are defacement (three cases), denial of service (16 cases), and doxing, which is defined as the practice of gathering and publicizing private information (four cases). These could be intended to coerce as well.

[9] Ministry of Foreign Affairs of the Russian Federation "Comment by the Information and Press Department on invitation for Montenegro to start talks on joining NATO," December 2, 2015. For the attribution of the

Chinese cyber operations show a continued focus on espionage, but potentially with some coercive intent as a secondary objective. China opposed a 2016 United States–Republic of Korea agreement to deploy the THAAD missile defense system to South Korea. China exerted coercive pressure, primarily through economic means, when it blocked South Korean companies from selling goods and services in China, but cyber intrusions also increased against South Korean government and private sector entities. These operations may have served an intelligence-gathering purpose, but also signaled Beijing's displeasure with the THAAD deployments.

Iranian cyber activity appears more focused on retaliating against regional neighbors and the West, rather than serving a direct coercive purpose. Cyberattacks against Saudi oil companies began with a destructive attack in 2012 that resulted in the loss of some 30,000 computers on the Saudi Arabian state oil company's (ARAMCO's) networks, but no discernable impact on operations. In 2017, the same malware resulted in similar damage to the petrochemical company Tasnee; that attack was followed by a subsequent attack on ARAMCO in August 2017 involving TRITON intrusion malware. In each case, there is not a discernible threat or desired behavior that Iran sought to bring about.

North Korea has routinely engaged in coercive acts in the physical world. In 2014, the pending release of a satirical movie—centered around a plot to kill North Korean leader Kim Jong-Un—prompted North Korea to lodge a vehement protest via the United Nations, and later resulted in a destructive attack on and release of internal documents from Sony Pictures Entertainment.

Our assessment of these cases indicates how the threat, threat actor, and the desired change in behavior is often unclear or ambiguous, though this ambiguity does not appear to prevent countries from pursuing these coercive campaigns. The Chinese case indicates that the cyber operations played a secondary role to economic pressure, while in the Iranian case, Iran does not appear to use cyber operations to coerce. Russia and North Korea, on the other hand, are more willing to do so.

As the growth and penetration of information technology leads to greater interdependencies across networks, systems and infrastructure sectors, cyber operations offer the potential of destructive consequences and will become more attractive tools of statecraft. In anticipation of these circumstances, the United States and its partners need to develop a richer understanding of how cyber coercion might emerge, build systems to provide warning of impending operations, and craft strategies to deter and respond.

---

denial of service attacks, see Maja Zivanovic, "Russia's Fancy Bear Hacks its Way Into Montenegro," *BalkanInsight,* March 5, 2018.

Acknowledgments

Our thanks to the leadership in RAND's Cyber and Intelligence Policy Center, Rich Girven and Sina Beaghley, and former center director John Parachini for their support and enthusiasm. We also thank Cynthia Dion-Schwarz for encouraging us to pursue the topic. Our thanks to Peter Roady for his review of an earlier draft, and to Michael Mazarr and Michael Sulmeyer for their thorough reviews. The authors wish to thank their colleague Bilyana Lilly for her work in identifying sources for attribution of Russian APTs. Any errors are the authors' responsibility alone.

We are grateful to the NATO Cooperative Cyber Defence Centre of Excellence for allowing us to present an earlier draft of this report at its annual conference, CyCon X, in May 2018 in Tallinn, Estonia.[1]

---

[1] Tomáš Minárik, Raik Jakschis, and Lauri Lindström, eds., *2018 10th International Conference on Cyber Conflict, CyConX: Maximising Effects*, Tallinn, Estonia: NATO CCD COE Publications, 2018.

Abbreviations

AMS	Academy of Military Science (China)
APT	advanced persistent threat
DDoS	distributed denial of service
DNI	Director of National Intelligence
FSB	Federal Security Service (Russia)
GSD	General Service Department (China)
ICA	Iranian Cyber Army
IRGC	Islamic Revolutionary Guards Corps
JCPOA	Joint Comprehensive Plan of Action
MSS	Ministry of State Security (China)
NATO	North Atlantic Treaty Organization
NDU	National Defense University (China)
NSD	Network Systems Department (China)
PLA	People's Liberation Army (China)
ROK	Republic of Korea (South Korea)
SCADA	Supervisory Control and Data Acquisition
SSF	Strategic Support Force
SVR	Foreign Intelligence Service (Russia)
THAAD	Terminal High Altitude Area Defense
TTP	tactics, techniques, and procedures

Introduction

In 2012, 30,000 computers at Saudi Arabia's state-owned oil company, ARAMCO, displayed images of a burning U.S. flag as their hard drives were wiped clean of all their stored data. In December 2015, the lights went out in parts of Western Ukraine, leaving almost 250,000 people without power for several hours. In 2016, Russian actors engaged in a broad range of cyber-enabled disinformation operations to sow discord and undermine the integrity of the U.S. presidential election. In 2017, WannaCry ransomware wreaked havoc on more than 200,000 computers worldwide, affecting numerous sectors, including the United Kingdom's National Health Service and the Russian railway system. With each passing year, the scope and scale of cyber operations grow while governments, companies, and the general public struggle to even keep up with the news, let alone defend themselves from these attacks. What motivates these attacks can vary from the misguided "can I hack into this network?"—to the truly malicious—"can we cause physical destruction through cyberspace?" The overriding motivation for many private sector data breaches appears to be financial, and for state-sponsored operations, the motivation appears to be espionage. In recent years, however, there have been large-scale and sometimes sophisticated attacks that appear to be politically motivated.[1]

As the development of more connected and interconnected systems and networks proceeds, the potential for actors to exert influence and impact the economic, political, and social wellbeing of other states is growing. Governments have grappled with how to protect themselves from these threats, as well as how to potentially harness the possibilities of cyberspace to achieve desired outcomes. The U.S. Director of National Intelligence, Dan Coats, has echoed his predecessor's concern about the cyberthreat to the United States, stating that "the warning lights are blinking red again" and that "the digital infrastructure that serves this country is literally under attack." He noted that the perpetrators of these attacks have multiple goals in mind, from stealing informa-

---

[1] Verizon, *2018 Data Breach Investigations Report: Tales of Dirty Deeds and Unscrupulous Activities*, 2018. The Council on Foreign Relations cyber operations tracker codes 237 out of 288 state-sponsored cyber operations as cases of cyber-enabled espionage as of February 5, 2019; see Council on Foreign Relations, "Cyber Operations Tracker," webpage, undated.

tion to "the possibility of a crippling cyberattack against our critical infrastructure."[2] Cyber operations have become another tool of statecraft that can be used for a variety of purposes. This report seeks to understand how cyber operations can play a role in inter-state relations in the space between cyber-enabled espionage and outright conflict. It asks whether and how states use cyber operations to coerce others and what can be done to prevent or mitigate such activity.

The difficulty of and lags in attribution, the relatively low barriers to entry, and the potential for deep psychological (if not physical) impacts make cyberspace an attractive method of exerting pressure on states when compared with other means that require greater technical and capital investments. One way that states may choose to use cyber operations, in between espionage and outright conflict, is by bringing pressure to bear that influences another state's decisionmaking. Simply stated, states may seek to coerce others with the threat of or limited use of cyber operations in order to motivate changes in behavior.

The method we employed was to begin with identifying specific instances where a cyber operation against another state or organization appeared motivated by more than theft of information, or had destructive consequences in line with other objectives. We then sought to understand how these operations fit into the broader context of state-to-state relations at the time, and we distilled how the operation in question may differ from the theoretical definition of coercion. The cases were chosen because of their potential to provide insights into a competition or conflict and the occurrence of cyber operations alongside other diplomatic, economic, or military activities. In each case, we address the following questions:

- Was there an explicit or implied threat aimed at another actor to coerce a change in behavior?
- Did the threat actor (coercer) make itself known to its intended victim?
- What were the broader political and economic circumstances surrounding the threatened action? Do these circumstances provide clues concerning potential coercive action?
- Were the cyber operations intended primarily to threaten or impose pain to motivate a change in behavior, or for some such other purpose as espionage or retaliation?

The cases were chosen because of their potential to provide insights into competition or conflict between two states, and the occurrence of cyber operations alongside other diplomatic, economic, or military activities. In addition, we reviewed two databases on cyber operations to identify potential cases and to determine the scale of

---

[2]   Dan Coats, "Statement for the Record: Worldwide Threat Assessment of the Intelligence Community," testimony before the Senate Select Committee on Intelligence, Washington, D.C.: Director of National Intelligence, May 11, 2017.

apparent cyber coercion as a subset of publicly known state-sponsored or -conducted cyber operations.[3] We found that cyber operations intended to coerce are a small subset of overall cyber operations globally. Valeriano and Maness's data set, covering 2001 through 2011, only identifies four cases of cyber operations seeking to change another state's behavior, and two of those are the same operation (the joint U.S.–Israeli cyber operation against the Iranian nuclear program). The Council on Foreign Relations' cyber operations tracker, covering 2005 to the present, does not code operations by apparent intent, but by using the attack type as a proxy for intent, we can see that only 23 of 288 operations resulted in data destruction or sabotage, compared with 237 cases of espionage.[4] Therefore, cyber operations are still predominantly used by states to spy on each other. Given the unclassified nature of this study, we did not have access to any private communications between the involved states or evidence of cyber activity that did not gain public attention through media coverage, official government pronouncements, or reports from cybersecurity researchers.

This report is organized as follows. In Chapter Two, we address the concept of cyber coercion and general considerations for how cyber coercion may occur compared with a theoretically pure definition, concluding with our definition. In Chapters Three through Six, we follow with an exploration of cyber operations attributed to Russia, China, Iran, and North Korea, respectively. For each country, we discuss government policy and doctrine on cyber operations—to the extent that they are known in open literature—followed by a description of the major advanced persistent threat (APT) cyber groups attributed to those governments. Finally, in Chapter Seven, we conclude by proposing areas for further exploration that will aid in deepening our understanding of how cyber operations can coerce, how states should think about developing indicators and warning, and how to craft deterrence and resilience strategies to counter cyber coercion.

---

[3] Valeriano, Brandon, and Ryan C. Maness, "The Dynamics of Cyber Conflict Between Rival Antagonists, 2001–11," *Journal of Peace Research*, Vol. 51, No. 3, 2014. The Council on Foreign Relations has compiled a data set covering 2005–2018; see Council on Foreign Relations, "Cyber Operations Tracker," webpage, undated.

[4] The other categories are defacement (three cases), denial of service (16 cases), and doxing, which is defined as the practice of gathering and publicizing private information (four cases). These could be intended to coerce as well.

CHAPTER TWO

Defining Coercion

In this chapter, we discuss the concept of coercion and point to how scholarly writing on cyber coercion is often inadequate and does not reflect how coercion occurs in practice. We conclude by providing a definition for cyber coercion and its characteristics.

Any discussion of coercion naturally begins with Thomas Schelling's seminal work, *Arms and Influence*. Schelling described two forms of coercion: active coercion (compellence) and passive coercion (deterrence).[1] The former involves the active use of force in some form to compel action by another, whereas the latter involves the threatened use of force to either motivate action or refrain from a particular action. The distinction is more of a continuum, as some states may combine compellence actions with the threat of more devastating consequences to accomplish their ends.

In recent years, popular, political, and academic discourses have tried to find appropriate analogies or comparable historical instances from other domains to explain cyberspace operations, the concepts of deterrence, or to distinguish cyberspace issues from other security issues.[2] This report begins with the premise that cyberspace as a domain is not fundamentally different than other domains when it comes to international relations. By this, we mean that states will seek to use cyber operations as one tool of statecraft,[3] just as they seek to use tools to further their interests such as military force, economic power, or social and humanitarian influence. The same principle applies to the use of cyber operations as a way to exert influence or pressure on others to shape behavior, deter adverse actions, and compel an actor to act (either another state, a multinational organization, or even a single individual). One group of researchers noted that coercion is "the use of threatened force, including the limited use of actual force to back up the threat, to induce an adversary to behave in differently than

---

[1]   Thomas C. Schelling, *Arms and Influence*, New Haven, Conn.: Yale University Press, 1966.

[2]   Joseph S. Nye, Jr., "Nuclear Lessons for Cyber Security?" *Strategic Studies Quarterly*, Vol. 5, No. 4, Winter 2011.

[3]   We use *cyber operations* as defined by the U.S. Department of Defense: "the employment of cyberspace capabilities where the primary purpose is to achieve objectives in or through cyberspace." We have chosen to use the more colloquial term "cyber operations" instead of "cyberspace operations." See U.S. Department of Defense, *DOD Dictionary of Military and Associated Terms*, undated.

it otherwise would."[4] This definition does not require a defined level of force: cyber weapons do not need to have the same potential to be credibly used to exert influence as nuclear or even conventional weapons, nor does the threatened use of cyber operations need to be explicit to have a coercive effect, as we seek to demonstrate in this report. The researchers' definition is also consistent with Schelling's, where he includes the notion of active coercion involving the coercer inflicting some punishment to demonstrate commitment, and putting the onus on the coerced to take action to forestall further punishment. In his formulation, "compellence, in contrast, usually involves *initiating* an action (or an irrevocable commitment to an action) that can cease, or become harmless, only if the opponent responds."[5]

Coercion in international relations is not the same as kidnapping, though some of the academic literature uses formulations that more closely resemble kidnapping than the dynamics of interstate relations. This difference is important for two reasons: 1) context is critical to understanding whether coercion is occurring; and 2) the potential for miscommunication between coercer and coerced can be significant, even if there is a longstanding relationship between states, as we shall see in some of the case studies in this report. In a kidnapping, there is usually an explicit demand, whether it is money or some other outcome, such as the release of political prisoners. The scholarly literature describes a logic for the dynamic between coercer and coerced: "if you do not do X, I will do Y."[6] Another form this takes is that a coercive action or threat "demands clarity in the expected result … [and to] be accompanied by some signal of urgency."[7] In reality, the demands are not always so clear. The threat actor may not make a clear threat or identify itself explicitly.

We articulate the difference between theory and observed practice as follows: coercion *in theory* requires one actor to make explicit demands of another that are tied to clear consequences in the event of noncompliance. Consequences can include inflicting pain or punishment to demonstrate commitment and signal that worse is to come if the threatened state or actor does not accede to the coercer's demands.[8] *In practice*, however, a coercing state may only make vague threats or even seek to covertly act to inflict some pain with the intent of motivating the coerced state to change its behavior. The specific desired behavior may not be clearly stated either. Observed practice is not

---

[4] David E. Johnson, Karl P. Mueller, and William H. Taft, *Conventional Coercion Across the Spectrum of Operations: The Utility of U.S. Military Forces in the Emerging Security Environment*, Santa Monica, Calif.: RAND Corporation, MR-1494-A, 2003, p. 8.

[5] Schelling, p. 72.

[6] Erica D. Borghard and Shawn W. Lonergan, "The Logic of Coercion in Cyberspace," *Security Studies*, Vol. 26. No. 3, 2017, pp. 433–34.

[7] Christopher Whyte, "Ending Cyber Coercion: Computer Network Attack, Exploitation and the Case of North Korea," *Comparative Strategy*, Vol. 35, No. 2, 2016.

[8] Schelling, p.171.

always entirely ambiguous: It could involve a clear demand, but an ill-defined threat. Or the threat could be stated clearly with a distinct desired outcome, but the threat actor may operate through a proxy to convey the threat, complicating the response. This observed practice of coercion makes it more difficult to recognize coercion in its early stages, or indeed potentially throughout much of the coercive campaign. This, in turn, complicates matters for the threatened state as it takes steps to counteract or blunt the threat.[9] In addition to this distinction between the theory and practice of cyber coercion, the two parties may not perceive the messages in the same way.[10]

Some scholars have noted that cyber coercion is less likely to achieve objectives because the coercive message will signal the threat and allow the coerced to respond or defend itself, reducing the effectiveness of the coercive measure.[11] These conclusions are based on assumptions that do not hold up under scrutiny. First, they assume that the coercive measure will be explicit and specific, to provide the coerced the chance to preempt the action or prepare its defenses. However, there is good reason to doubt that the threat will be specific enough to allow a reasonable defensive action in practice. Additionally, many nations' growing vulnerability to cyberattacks, particularly in more technologically advanced societies, means that the prospective attack surface is so large that adequate preparation is unlikely. The emergence of the "Internet of Things" and increasingly networked operational technology systems portends even greater vulnerability in the future. Second, the assumption is that the coercer will signal the means it will use to threaten an opponent. The coercer, however, does not have to state the exact means that will be employed to be credible. The coerced merely has to believe that the coercer has the capability to inflict harm—in any way it is able to do so—without stating "and I will do so with my cyber armies." For this report, therefore, we define *cyber coercion* as the threat (implied or explicit) or limited use of cyber operations to motivate a change in behavior by another actor that may involve cyber operations on their own or in conjunction with other coercive actions.

As a final note, we are not advancing an argument about the likely success of cyber coercion. Indeed, several scholars have already addressed the seemingly low rate of success for cyber coercion.[12] Successful cyber coercion results from either the credible threat or some elements of a successful cyber operation with a change in behavior. Even in cases where the operation itself achieves its proximate aims (e.g., limited damage to critical infrastructure), it appears that behavioral changes are few, whether because the

---

[9] This circumstance also potentially reduces the effectiveness of a coercive threat.

[10] Robert Jervis, *Perception and Misperception in International Politics*, Princeton, N.J.: Princeton University Press, 1976.

[11] Erik Gartzke, "The Myth of Cyberwar: Bringing War in Cyberspace Back Down to Earth," *International Security*, Vol. 38, No. 2, 2013.

[12] Benjamin Jensen, Brandon Valeriano, and Ryan C. Maness, "Cyber Compellence: Applying Coercion in the Information Age," undated; Borghard and Lonergan, 2017.

actor carrying out the operation overestimated the likely impact or because it underestimated the capacity of the adversary to withstand pain. Despite this poor track record, however, states persist in developing cyber capabilities and appear to believe, rightly or wrongly, that there is promise in cyber coercion. Therefore, we can expect states to continue to pursue coercive actions through cyberspace, and even increasingly turn to cyber operations to coerce.

CHAPTER THREE

Russia

The first of our cases examines Russian cyber operations in the context of its ongoing conflict with Ukraine and its attempts to dissuade Montenegro from joining both the North Atlantic Treaty Organization (NATO) and the European Union (EU). This case shows that Russian cyber operations are intended to coerce changes in behavior toward shunning the West and accommodating Russia's worldview.

Russian cyber operations have gained prominence over the past decade, beginning with distributed denial of service attacks against large segments of the Estonian economy and government in 2007, and as part of the country's conflict with Georgia in 2008, which some sources have attributed to the Russian government or to "patriotic hackers" acting on the government's behalf.[1] Since at least 2016, Russian cyber actors have also engaged in large-scale and far-reaching disinformation campaigns and interference in elections, from the United States to Germany and France.[2] Russian actors, some more closely affiliated with the government and others playing a more ambiguous role, have established online personas on multiple Internet platforms, including Twitter and Facebook, to disseminate falsified news stories and develop narratives sympathetic to Russia's views.[3] In the midst of such campaigns, it appears that Russia has also started to use cyber operations as a coercive tool. In this section we explore two instances of potential Russian cyber coercion, in Ukraine and Montenegro. Russian disinformation campaigns may also be coercive measures, intended to destabilize other countries and either promote more pro-Russian parties and social movements, or motivate current elites to accommodate Russian demands. We have not explicitly addressed those campaigns, because Russian disinformation appears designed to sow

---

[1] Joshua Davis, "Hackers Take Down the Most Wired Country in Europe," *Wired*, August 21, 2008; David Hollis, "Cyberwar Case Study: Georgia 2008," *Small Wars Journal*, 2011.

[2] FireEye iSight Intelligence, *Russia's APT 28 Strategically Evolves Its Cyber Operations*, January 11, 2017.

[3] Dan Coats, 2017; and Indictment, *United States v. Internet Research Agency*, Case 1:18-cr-00032-DLF (D.D.C. February 16, 2018).

general discord and undermine political and social cohesion, rather than motivate specific changes in behavior.[4]

Russian national strategy and policy take a broad view of the role of cyber operations. Russia's 2015 *National Security Strategy* notes that "in the struggle for influence in the international arena, the whole spectrum of political, financial, economic and information instruments is involved."[5] Its Information Security Doctrine lays out the Russian view of a state under siege in the information sphere by outside forces that seek to undermine the "sovereignty, political and social stability, [and] the territorial integrity of the Russian Federation and its allies."[6] Russia's approach to countering this state of affairs is to conceive of cyber operations as a subelement of broader information warfare, combining elements of psychological operations, electronic warfare, and network attack.[7] Russian military thinking speaks of information warfare as encompassing actions that can impact information systems (i.e., information technology [IT] networks), but with the ultimate aim of undermining those systems or "producing mass psychological effects with the aim of destabilizing society and the state or coercing the state to make decisions in the interests of the opposing side."[8] Although Russia sees its adversaries conducting such operations against it, these writings indicate how Russia thinks about the potential role for cyber operations in its own operations as well. One recent study termed the Russian (and Chinese) approach as "comprehensive coercion."[9] Russian doctrine and security policies therefore recognize the potential to coerce with cyber operations.

Cybersecurity firms have attributed more than half a dozen APTs to Russia. Russian APTs have targeted commercial companies, government agencies, political par-

---

[4]   For more on disinformation campaigns, see Bodine-Baron, Elizabeth, Todd C. Helmus, Andrew Radin, and Elina Treyger, *Countering Russian Social Media Influence*, Santa Monica, Calif.: RAND Corporation, RR-2740-RC, 2018.

[5]   President of the Russian Federation, "Decree of the President of the Russian Federation from 31 December 2015, No. 683, About the National Security Strategy of the Russian Federation [Указ Президента Российской Федерации от 31.12.2015 г. № 683, О Стратегии национальной безопасности Российской Федерации]," December 31, 2015.

[6]   President of the Russian Federation, "Decree of the President of the Russian Federation from 5 December 2016, No. 646, About the Approval of the Doctrine of Information Security of the Russian Federation [Указ Президента Российской Федерации от 05.12.2016 г., № 646, Об утверждении Доктрины информационной безопасности Российской Федерации]," December 5, 2016.

[7]   Connell, Michael, and Sarah Vogler, Russia's Approach to Cyber Warfare, Arlington, Va.: CNA Analysis and Solutions, September 2016, p. 2.

[8]   Ministry of Defense of the Russian Federation, Conceptual Views on the Activities of the Armed Forces of the Russian Federation in the Information Space [Концептуальные взгляды на деятельность Вооруженных Сил Российской Федерации в информационном пространстве], 2011.

[9]   Thomas G. Mahnken, Ross Babbage, and Toshi Yoshihara, *Countering Comprehensive Coercion: Competitive Strategies Against Authoritarian Political Warfare*, Washington, D.C.: Center for Strategic and Budgetary Assessments, May 30, 2018.

ties, and international organizations around the world, and have targeted multiple sectors, from pharmaceuticals to finance. The Russian government agencies engaged in cyber operations, whether for espionage purposes or more active measures, include the military's Main Directorate, the Federal Security Service (FSB), and the Foreign Intelligence Service (SVR). The CyberBerkut group, which has been active in Ukraine, claims it is a pro-Russian "hacktivist" group, but some suspect it is a front or direct proxy for the Russian government.[10]

Russia and Ukraine

Russians historically see Ukraine as a part of the border region of Russian territory, rather than as a separate geographic and political entity (in Russian, Ukraine roughly means "on the border"). This is especially true about the Crimean Peninsula, which was a gift to the Ukrainian Soviet Socialist Republic during Nikita Khrushchev's tenure as leader of the Soviet Union, and which still serves as the home port for the Russian Navy's Black Sea fleet.[11] Ukraine's negotiations to conclude a political and trade deal with the EU in 2013 threatened to put Ukraine more squarely in the West's sphere of influence.

Protests erupted in Ukraine's capital, Kyiv, after then–President Viktor Yanukovich reversed course on the deal with the EU. Police moved in to confront the protesters and violence ensued, resulting in dozens of deaths.[12] In the aftermath of these protests, Russian soldiers seized Crimea and pro-Russian groups in Eastern Ukraine began to seize control of government institutions, prompting the government to respond militarily. Following the election of President Petro Poroshenko in May 2014, fighting continued and despite a ccasefire negotiated in February 2015, the conflict is ongoing. Russia's apparent actions to destabilize Ukraine through various means including cyber operations, supporting proxy fighters, and sending military forces into Eastern Ukraine stem from a desire to keep Ukraine in Russia's orbit and prevent Ukraine's further integration with the West.[13]

In the midst of the horrific fighting and civilian suffering, particularly in Eastern Ukraine, the country suffered the first significant cyberattack on its electric grid in December 2015. The attack affected approximately 250,000 customers for some hours, but appeared to have no lasting damage despite targeting the Supervisory Control and Data Acquisition (SCADA) controllers that control mechanical processes in addition

---

[10] ThreatConnect, "Belling the Bear," updated October 7, 2016.

[11] Martin McCauley, The Soviet Union 1917-1991, London, UK: Longman, 1993.

[12] Anne Applebaum, "Why Does Putin Want to Control Ukraine? Ask Stalin," Washington Post, October 20, 2017.

[13] Daniel Treisman, "Why Putin Took Crimea: The Gambler in the Kremlin," Foreign Affairs, April 18, 2016.

to business-system workstations and servers.[14] The malware employed in the cyber-attack was a set of tools, including the BlackEnergy Trojan and the KillDisk eraser, that targeted at least three geographically diverse regional power substations.[15] The impact on the energy sector received the most attention, as the attack occurred during Ukraine's cold winter season, but the cyber operations against Ukraine also impacted the media, finance, and transportation sectors. Cybersecurity researchers have attributed the use of BlackEnergy and the actions in Ukraine to the Sandworm intrusion set, which many believe is a Russian hacker group.[16] The Ukrainian government has been more explicit in tying these activities to Russian security services. Attacks on various sectors continued in 2016, including another attack that hit the Kyiv transmission station almost exactly a year after the December 2015 attacks. That outage lasted barely an hour.

The Russian government has not claimed responsibility for these cyberattacks and routinely denies involvement in cyber operations against other countries, reminding audiences of evidence that the United States, in particular, has engaged in the widespread use of cyber operations.[17] The Russian government did not appear to make explicit demands of the Ukrainian government or public, either in advance of the attacks or afterward. In the context of the broader conflict, however, Russia's strategy appears to include establishing facts on the ground through the maneuver of military forces and use of proxies, spreading disinformation to attempt to portray the West and pro-Western Ukrainians as enemies of the Ukrainian people, and using cyber operations to reinforce that messaging. Cyber operations in this context appear to aim toward broadly destabilizing political and social cohesion in Ukraine.[18] Russian actions, therefore, aim to force the Ukrainian government to acquiesce to Russian influence and halt its integration with the West.

---

[14] Michael J. Assante, "Confirmation of a Coordinated Attack on the Ukrainian Power Grid," SANS Industrial Control Systems, January 9, 2016.

[15] Andy Greenberg, "How an Entire Nation Became Russia's Test Lab for Cyberwar," *Wired*, June 20, 2017.

[16] John Hultquist, "Sandworm Team and the Ukrainian Power Authority Attacks," FireEye, January 7, 2016. Sandworm is likely the same group known as Quedagh and Voodoo Bear. Although some, such as cybersecurity company Crowdstrike, have attributed the group's actions to the Russian Federation, its actions in Ukraine have not tied it directly to the work of a government agency or affiliate (e.g., APT 28 or APT 29).

[17] Ministry of Foreign Affairs of the Russian Federation, "Comment by Foreign Ministry Spokesperson Maria Zakharova on New Threats of Sanctions from the United States," December 28, 2016.

[18] There is also speculation that the Russians are using the conflict with Ukraine to "test" its cyber capabilities in a real-world laboratory, as a prelude to potential use against other countries (e.g., the United States). Although this may be a collateral benefit, there is little public evidence to support this as the primary reason.

Montenegro's Assimilation into the West

The emergence of Montenegro as an independent country, and ultimately a member of NATO, provides another instructive case of cyber coercion. A small Balkan country with a population of approximately 650,000, Montenegro gained independence from Serbia in 2006. Shortly after gaining independence, Montenegro joined the NATO Partnership for Peace program.[19] In 2008, it submitted its application to the European Union to begin membership accession talks, followed in 2009 by the start of NATO accession through the Membership Action Plan process. Montenegro's actions to deepen its ties to the West have drawn criticism from Moscow. Russia's Ministry of Foreign Affairs called the December 2015 invitation to start accession talks from NATO "additional destabilizing consequences for the system of Euro-Atlantic security … This new round of the Alliance's expansion directly affects the interests of the Russian Federation and forces us to respond accordingly."[20] Dmitry Peskov, President Putin's spokesman, went further, saying that "the continued eastward expansion of NATO and NATO's military infrastructure cannot but result in retaliatory actions from the east, i.e., from the Russian side, in terms of ensuring security and supporting the parity of interests," though he did not elaborate on what form those actions would take.[21]

Russia signaled its opposition to Montenegro's NATO membership with more than just words. The Ministry of Foreign Affairs called for a referendum in Montenegro while also pushing for Balkan neutrality. In October 2015, the Montenegrin opposition party Democratic Front led protests against the ruling party of Prime Minister Milo Djukanovic, who in turn accused the Democratic Front of trying to stop Montenegro's NATO accession.[22] Djukanovic voiced his suspicions that Russia was supporting the opposition, though he did not present any evidence to back up his claims.[23] A year later, on the eve of parliamentary elections, the police arrested 14 Serbian citizens and six Montenegrins who were allegedly planning to claim victory for the Democratic Front and seize the parliament. Montenegrin authorities asserted that the attempted coup was supported by Serbian nationalists and Russian intelligence officers.[24] At the same time, websites for Montenegrin government ministries, media, and the ruling

---

[19] The Partnership for Peace program is NATO's program to engage in bilateral cooperation with non–NATO countries in the Euro-Atlantic area. NATO, "Partnership for Peace Programme," webpage, 2017.

[20] Ministry of Foreign Affairs of the Russian Federation, "Comment by the Information and Press Department on Invitation for Montenegro to Start Talks on Joining NATO," December 2, 2015.

[21] NATO Invitation to Montenegro Prompts Russia Warning, *BBC News*, December 2, 2015.

[22] Peter Komnenic, "Thousands Protest Against Montenegro's Government," *Reuters*, October 18, 2015.

[23] "Montenegro: Caught in the Midst of the East-West Conflict," Deutsche Welle, October 23, 2015.

[24] Reuf Bajrović, Vesko Garčević, and Richard Kraemer, *Hanging by a Thread: Russia's Strategy of Destabilization in Montenegro*, Philadelphia: Foreign Policy Research Institute, June 2018, p. 9.

Democratic Party of Socialists were subjected to distributed denial of service (DDoS) attacks.[25] Cybersecurity firm TrendMicro also determined that APT 28, a Russia-attributed intrusion set, engaged in a phishing campaign against the Montenegrin parliament. Russia may have intended to support the alleged coup and create additional confusion during a particularly tense time. The phishing campaign continued in 2017, as the date for Montenegro's NATO membership drew closer. The phishing emails sent by APT 28 clearly sought to capitalize on the interest in NATO accession, and included email attachments with titles like "NATO_secretary_meeting.doc" and subject lines such as "Draft schedule for British army groups' visit to Montenegro."[26] Phishing emails by themselves are not directly coercive in nature; destructive attacks do not necessarily result from simply clicking on a link or opening an attachment with malicious code. These emails do, however, provide a foothold in a network of interest. The DDoS attacks may have also sought to signal general displeasure with the direction in which the Montenegrin government was headed. Subsequent phishing campaigns occurred in February 2017, and again in June after Montenegro officially joined NATO.

Russian cyber operations against Ukraine and Montenegro show the importance of understanding the context in which conflict occurs. Analysis that examines cyber operations in isolation will fail to identify the implicit outcomes Russia seeks and has expressed multiple times. In the first case we explored here, Russia is not looking for Ukraine to undertake a single, specific action to forestall future cyber coercion; rather, it is executing a broader campaign to prevent Ukraine's integration with the West. The case of Montenegro's NATO accession is more clearly coercive, because Russia voiced official opposition to the accession while supporting other measures to undermine the political consensus in Montenegro. The implication of the verbal threats coupled with the actions in-country through proxies and cyberspace indicate that the desired outcome was for Montenegro to draw back from further Western integration. Russia made explicit that it opposed both Ukraine and Montenegro developing closer ties to the West and used various means to undermine those governments, including the use of cyber operations.

---

[25] Jonathan Keane, "Hackers Tried to Disrupt the Parliamentary Elections in Montenegro," *Digital Trends*, October 17, 2016.

[26] Maja Zivanovic, "Russia's Fancy Bear Hacks its Way Into Montenegro," *BalkanInsight*, March 5, 2018; Chris Bing, "APT28 Targeted Montenegro's Government Before It Joined NATO, Researchers Say," CyberScoop, June 6, 2017.

CHAPTER FOUR

China

Chinese cyber operations predominantly serve the purpose of espionage against other states. The Council on Foreign Relations database of cyber operations identifies 99 of 102 Chinese cyber operations as being focused on espionage.[1] This focus is not surprising, given the country's unrelenting drive to promote Chinese economic development, but the absence of any attempts to coerce others, even in such disputes such as that in the South China Sea, is surprising. China addresses cyber operations in its strategy and doctrine as part of a shift in People's Liberation Army (PLA) thinking, toward considering information as a strategic resource instrumental to winning future wars. Prompted by its observations of United States' success in Operation Desert Storm, the PLA shifted its priorities toward "informatization." The broader emphasis on informatization catalyzed developments in information warfare and, more specifically, network operations.[2] In this chapter, we examine a case where China used cyber operations—along with economic and diplomatic pressure—to oppose deployment of U.S. air defense systems to South Korea, to see whether the cyber operations served a coercive purpose.

PLA analysts divide cyber operations into three broad categories: network reconnaissance, network attack and defense operations, and network deterrence.[3] *Network reconnaissance* consists of operations conducted to gather information and expose vulnerabilities in the adversary's information systems. According to the 2013 edition of the Academy of Military Science (AMS) *Science of Military Strategy*, network reconnaissance is "the most common form of military struggle in the network domain today."[4]

---

[1] The Council on Foreign Relations database is available for download from Council on Foreign Relations, undated.

[2] "Network operations" comes closest to reflecting Chinese terminology for the technical aspects of a broader concept around informatization or information conflict. The term is closest to the former U.S. doctrinal term "cyberspace operations."

[3] Shou Xiaosong, ed., *The Science of Military Strategy* [战略学], Beijing, China: Military Science Press, 2013, pp. 192–194. Major General Shou Xiaosong is director of the War Theory and Strategic Research Department of the Academy of Military Science.

[4] Shou Xiaosong, 2013.

Network attack and *defense operations* are defined as operational activities carried out to damage enemy network systems and information in order to degrade their functional utilities while protecting one's own.[5] These operations are the highest form of military struggle in the network domain.[6] *Network deterrence* is described as actions taken to display network offensive and defensive capabilities to forcefully prevent an opponent from carrying out large-scale network attacks.[7] As the following section explains, the Chinese conception of deterrence is different from the U.S. interpretation, as it includes both elements of deterrence and compellence.

While the PLA often describes network operations in the context of large-scale combat, the same principles are applicable to peacetime. A common tenet in PLA discussions on network operations is the blurring of boundaries between peace and war. As opposed to the traditional Western division of the two into distinct stages, the PLA tends to view military competition as part of what China scholars John Costello and Joe McReynolds describe as an "'omnipresent' struggle, a Maoist-Marxist-Leninist paradigm that sees a broad political front in an enduring clash of political systems and ideologies."[8] The same concept applies to the cyberspace. In the words of Ye Zheng, an expert in information warfare at AMS, "the strategic game in the cyberspace is not limited by time and space, does not distinguish between peace and war, and has no frontline and homefront."[9]

This continuum is evident in PLA juxtapositions of nondestructive network reconnaissance and destructive network attack. According to the 2013 *Science of Military Strategy*, "[its] operating tenets are essentially identical; the means and methods of network reconnaissance usually are the means and methods of network attack."[10] As McReynolds explains, PLA network reconnaissance activities in peacetime "incrementally put China into a superior tactical position should conflict ever break out" and, while "provocative," "are unlikely to lead to direct conflict in and of themselves."[11] Should "conflict […] break out, China will be in a better position than they otherwise

---

[5]   Shou Xiaosong, 2013.

[6]   Shou Xiaosong, 2013.

[7]   Shou Xiaosong, 2013.

[8]   John Costello and Joe McReynolds, *China's Strategic Support Force: A Force for a New Era*, Washington, D.C.: National Defense University Press, October 2018, p. 45.

[9]   Ye Zheng, "A Discussion of the Innate Characteristics, the Composition of Forces, and the Included Forms" [论网络空间战略博弈的本质特征，力量构成与内容形势], China Information Security [中国信息安全], August 2014. Ye Zheng served as the director of the Informationized Operations Research Office at the AMS Operational Theory and Regulations Department.

[10] Shou, 2013, p. 192.

[11] Joe McReynolds, "China's Evolving Perspectives on Network Warfare: Lessons from the Science of Military Strategy," *China Brief*, Vol. 15, No. 8, April 16, 2015.

would; if it does not, they will have incrementally gained much of what they desire without a fight."[12]

In addition to the blurring of lines between peace and war in cyberspace, China also blurs the lines between the military and civilian realms. Aside from military and government capabilities, the 2013 *Science of Military Strategy* notes that civilians capable of spontaneous network attack and defense could be employed in network operations.[13] Unlike more-traditional concepts of warfare, this is a testament to the expansiveness of cyberspace as a domain; military and civilian actors will engage in cyber competition and conflict, and this will likely spill into the civilian domain.

There are multiple APTs attributed to China, including government entities and potentially aligned proxies or front groups. The first public attribution was a February 2013 Mandiant report, which identified cyber operations conducted by the PLA's 3rd General Service Department's (GSD) 2nd Bureau.[14] Since then, FireEye (which acquired Mandiant in 2013) has attributed at least nine APTs to China, though not all with attribution tying them to the Chinese government.[15] The primary government agencies operating cyber units in China are the PLA and the Ministry of State Security. Previously, the 3rd and 4th GSDs housed the PLA's cyber operations units, but in 2015 the PLA restructured to place these capabilities along with space, electronic warfare, and psychological warfare units into a new Strategic Support Force (SSF).[16] The SSF's Network Systems Department (NSD) oversees cyber operations, but encompasses a broader array of activities than the United States Cyber Command. Reflecting Chinese doctrine and thinking that conceives of the information sphere as a central area for conflict to play out, the SSF NSD also has responsibility for space, electromagnetic, psychological, and some kinetic operations.[17] The Ministry of State Security (MSS), on the other hand, is even more secretive, and it is difficult to ascertain its role in cyber operations.

The U.S. Department of Justice indicted three employees of a Chinese company called Boyusec on charges of cyber espionage in 2017. Although the federal prosecutors took pains to note that they were not making claims about Boyusec's affiliation or connections, if any, to the Chinese government, others in the private sector have indicated they believe Boyusec was working as cyber "guns for hire" for the MSS.[18] Recorded

---

[12] McReynolds, 2015.

[13] Shou Xiaosong, 2013, p. 196.

[14] Dan McWhorter, "Mandiant Exposes APT1—One of China's Cyber Espionage Units & Releases 3,000 Indicators," FireEye, February 19, 2013.

[15] FireEye, "Advanced Persistent Threat Groups: Who's Who of Cyber Threat Actors," webpage, undated.

[16] Costello and McReynolds, 2018.

[17] Costello and McReynolds, 2018, p. 4.

[18] Elias Groll, "Feds Quietly Reveal Chinese State-Backed Hacking Operations," *Foreign Policy*, November 30, 2017.

Future, a cyber threat intelligence provider, linked APT 3 to the MSS with "a high degree of confidence" earlier in 2017.[19]

Western analysts note that the Chinese term *weishe* [威慑] commonly translates into "deterrence" in English, but that the term also embodies elements of both "deterrence" and "compellence."[20] According to the 2005 edition of the AMS *Science of Military Strategy*, "deterrence plays two basic roles: one is to dissuade the opponent from doing something through deterrence, the other is to persuade the opponent what ought to be done through deterrence, and both demand the opponent to submit to the deterrer's volition."[21] *Weishe* could be perceived as "the rough equivalent to [...] Schelling's broader concept of coercion, which includes deterrence and compellence."[22]

On one hand, PLA strategists are cognizant of the potential *weishe* applications of network operations. Many view network operations as a potent tool for subduing adversaries without fighting, a longstanding principle of Chinese strategic culture. As early as 2000, one PLA strategist wrote of the possibility of "[sending] a message to the enemy through computer network attack, forcing the enemy to give up without fighting."[23] A 2009 Chinese National Defense University (NDU) textbook notes that information operations, including network operations, can "sow fear and panic amongst the enemy" and "compel adversaries away from rash activities."[24] Senior Colonel Cao Zhengrong, a researcher at the PLA Nanjing Command College, opined that network attacks could paralyze a nation's economy and sow societal disorder, allowing one country to impose its will upon the other.[25] Notably, Cao believes this is possible

---

[19] Insikt Group, "Recorded Future Research Concludes Chinese Ministry of State Security Behind APT3," Recorded Future, May 17, 2017.

[20] Dean Cheng, "Chinese Views on Deterrence," *Joint Force Quarterly*, No. 60, 2011; Michael S. Chase and Arthur Chan, *China's Evolving Approach to "Integrated Strategic Deterrence,"* Santa Monica, Calif.: RAND Corporation, RR-1366-TI, 2016, pp. 4–5.

[21] Peng Guangqian and Yao Youzhi, *The Science of Military Strategy* [战略学], Beijing, China: Military Science Press, 2005, p. 215.

[22] Chase and Chan, 2016, pp. 4–5. For the sake of accurate interpretation of Chinese primary sources, this section will retain the term *weishe* when describing Chinese views of network-based deterrence.

[23] Wang Houqing and Zhang Xingye, *The Science of Military Campaigns* [战役学], Beijing, China: National Defense University Press, 2000, pp. 173–174, referenced in James Mulvenon, "PLA Computer Network Operations: Scenarios, Doctrine, Organizations, and Capability," in Roy Kamphausen, David Lai, and Andrew Scobell, eds., *Beyond the Strait: PLA Missions Other than Taiwan*, Carlisle, Penn.: Strategic Studies Institute, 2009, p. 257. Lieutenant General Wang Houqing and Lieutenant General Zhang Xingye previously served as vice presidents of the PLA National Defense University.

[24] Yuan Wenxian, ed., *Lectures on Joint Campaign Information Operations* [联合战役信息作战教程], Beijing, China: Military Science Press, 2009, p. 109. Yuan Wenxian served as the director of the Information Operations and Command Training Teaching and Research Department of the PLA National Defense University.

[25] Cao Zhengrong, Wu Renbo, and Sun Jianjun, eds., *Informationized Joint Operations* [信息化联合作战], Beijing: People's Liberation Army Press, 2006, Chapter 2.

in both wartime and peacetime, suggesting the applicability of cyber coercion below the threshold of outright war.[26]

On the other hand, as the *Science of Military Strategy* alludes, the extent of which network-based *weishe* is feasible in practice appears to be a subject of debate within the PLA:

> "Although [*weishe*] is important component of military struggle in the network domain, there is nonetheless very great diversity in the understanding of network [*weishe*], and *both the theory and practice of network deterrence await further development and perfection.*"[27]

PLA strategists identify several disadvantages of network-based *weishe*. Chief among those is that the ambiguous nature of cyber operations may reduce the efficacy of *weishe*.[28] Successful *weishe* results from effective signaling—the adversary must first be cognizant of the source and motivation of deterrence and coercion activities for it to take actions expected by the attackers. Other shortcomings of network-based *weishe* identified by PLA strategists include the following:

- Unlike nuclear war and conventional war, the destructive potential of a major cyberwar is currently unknown—its *weishe* value is primarily based on conjecture.
- Cyber operations are a complex, dynamic process of continual interaction between two adversaries, rendering difficult the measurement of their *weishe* effect.
- Although cyber operations could be tailored for specific tasks, their operational scope could be difficult to contain. There is high risk of escalation and expansion. One such case is the inadvertent spread of a destructive computer virus to a neutral party.
- Network-based *weishe* is less effective in countries with little to no information network infrastructure.
- Operational command and control protocols for cyber operations are underdeveloped, a problem exacerbated by the diverse range of actors involved in the cyberspace.[29]

It appears that China is taking a more circumspect approach to using cyber operations for coercive purposes, focusing largely on stealing data or silencing critics of the

---

[26] Costello and McReynolds, 2018, p. 45.

[27] Shou, 2013, p. 194. Italics added by authors for emphasis.

[28] Shou, 2013, p. 190.

[29] Yuan Yi, "A Rough Analysis of the Characteristics, Categories, and Utility of Deterrence in the Cyberspace [浅析网络空间威慑的特征，类型，和运用要点]," *China Information Security*, No. 11, 2015. Yuan Yi is a researcher at the Academy of Military Science Operational Theory and Regulations Research Department.

regime. China may, however, seek to expand its use of cyber operations to coerce in the future.

Some Chinese thinkers have broached the idea of cyber operations serving a coercive purpose, noting that the very act of infiltrating an adversary's network could serve a coercive purpose. According to Major General Wang Zhengde, former head of the PLA Information Engineering University, network reconnaissance activities could signal to adversaries that their networks are exposed, leading them to adopt actions favorable to the aggressor.[30] In this context, the cyber espionage activities that make up the majority of Chinese activities in cyberspace could be perceived as tools of coercion as well, but are likely secondary effects at best and not their primary objective.

Chinese Response to THAAD Deployments in South Korea

On February 7, 2016, U.S. and South Korean officials announced plans to formally discuss the possibility of deploying the Terminal High Altitude Area Defense (THAAD) missile defense system in South Korea to bolster missile defense in the face of growing North Korean missile capabilities.[31] From the outset, Beijing repeatedly and vehemently opposed the deployment.[32] The source of Beijing's enmity reportedly lay in the system's potential to alter the regional security balance, as well as its component X-band AN/TPY-2 radar, which, due to its detection range of almost 3,000 miles, Beijing feared would allow the United States to monitor military activity deep within China and undermine its nuclear deterrent.[33]

Once the decision to proceed with the THAAD deployment was announced in July 2016, Beijing's tone escalated sharply. The following months saw Beijing carry out an aggressive campaign to publicly denounce the deployment through official channels.[34] In the economic sphere, it engaged in an unofficial campaign of economic coercion by blocking market access to South Korean goods and services in key industries.[35] All told, the South Korea–based Hyundai Research Institute estimated the THAAD

---

[30] Wang Zhengde, Information Confrontation Theory [信息对抗论], Military Science Publishing House, 2007, chapter 11. Aside from serving as president of the PLA Information Engineering University—a leading center of information warfare research—Wang Zhengde also served in the leadership of the General Staff Department's Third Department, the PLA organization responsible for network espionage.

[31] Anna Fifield, "South Korea, U.S. to Start Talks on Anti-Missile System," *Washington Post*, February 7, 2016.

[32] For in-depth examinations of China's response to THAAD, see Ethan Meick and Nargiza Salidjanova, *China's Response to U.S.-South Korean Missile Defense System Deployment and its Implications*, U.S.-China Economic and Security Review Commission, July 26, 2017; and Michael D. Swaine, "Chinese Views on South Korea's Deployment of THAAD," *China Leadership Monitor*, No. 52, Winter 2017.

[33] Michael Martina and Greg Torode, "Chinese Wary Over U.S. THAAD Missile System Because Capabilities Unknown, Experts Say," *Reuters*, April 3, 2017.

[34] Meick and Salidjanova, 2017.

[35] Bonnie S. Glaser, Daniel G. Sofio, and David A. Parker, "The Good, the THAAD, and the Ugly," *Foreign Affairs*, February 15, 2017.

controversy cost South Korea over $7.5 billion in economic losses in 2017.[36] Not until October 31, 2017, did Beijing and Seoul announce steps to repair bilateral relations. Although Beijing failed to compel Seoul to abandon THAAD altogether, it did manage to force South Korea's acquiescence to the so-called "three *nos*"—no additional deployment of THAAD systems, no participation in a U.S. missile defense network, and no establishment of a trilateral military alliance with the United States and Japan.[37]

During the THAAD dispute, as part of its campaign to coerce South Korea into shifting its stance on the missile defense system, China utilized not only political and economic levers but also appeared to leverage cyber intrusions. U.S.-based cybersecurity firm FireEye alleged that cyberespionage groups linked to Chinese military and intelligence agencies launched multiple attacks on South Korean government and commercial entities in response to Seoul's decision to deploy THAAD.[38] While Chinese hackers have long targeted South Korea, security experts tracked a discernable uptick in the number and intensity of cyber operations in the weeks following Seoul's confirmation of deployment of the missile defense system, suggesting, in the words of FireEye executive and former U.S. Indo-Pacific Command commander ADM Patrick Walsh, a "clear correlation" between cyber operations and THAAD deployment.[39] In response to FireEye's allegations, Beijing issued a blanket denial. The Chinese Ministry of National Defense declared that Beijing consistently opposed hacking, while maintaining that China was a longtime victim of cyberattacks.[40] The aim of these operations may have been to signal Chinese displeasure with the decision and to exert pressure to coerce the South to reverse the decision, but it is unlikely these operations were significant factors in the South Korean government's decisionmaking.

Beijing's response to the THAAD deployment is an example of cyber espionage used not just for intelligence gathering but also for coercive purposes to affect the decisions of another state. Individual cases of cyber espionage may not draw notice, but a sudden surge in the aggregate number of cyberintrusions will. Although there were no explicit demands tied to this set of cyber operations, such factors as the timing of the attacks, Beijing's highly publicized and increasing escalatory denouncements, the involvement of hackers linked with Chinese military and intelligence, and the specific targeting of THAAD-relevant Republic of Korea (ROK) organizations suggest an implicit demand. That being said, even if the cyber intrusions served a coercive pur-

---

[36] "S. Korea, China to Be Affected by THAAD Fall Out: Think Tank," *Yonhap News Agency*, May 3, 2017.

[37] Park Byong-su, "South Korea's 'Three No's' Announcement Key to Restoring Relations with China," *Hankyoreh*, November 2, 2017

[38] Jonathan Cheng and Josh Chin, "China Hacked South Korea Over Missile Defense, U.S. Firm Says," *Wall Street Journal*, April 21, 2017.

[39] Yeo Jun-suk, "China Launches Cyberattacks Against South Korea in Protest of THAAD: Former US Navy Commander," *Korea Herald*, April 27, 2017.

[40] Yeo Jun-suk, 2017.

pose, they likely only played a supporting role in influencing the ROK decisionmaking calculus when placed within the context of such larger issues as the deteriorating bilateral relationship and the significant economic losses incurred from economic coercion.

Given the geopolitical dynamics in the Asia-Pacific region stemming from Chinese economic growth, continued disputes with countries over claims in the South China Sea, and the security situation in Northeast Asia, one might expect China to seek to exert its influence over its neighbors using all available tools, including cyber operations. The THAAD case points to a more focused use of cyber operations, predominantly for espionage. This indicates that China derives the greatest benefit from using cyber operations to learn more about other countries, companies, and organizations' plans and intellectual property. FireEye concluded that the two primary reasons for conducting cyber operations against Southeast Asian countries were to "steal intellectual property and inside information from leading companies, and obtain intelligence on rival governments during long-running political disputes, especially those involving the disputed South China Sea."[41]

---

[41] FireEye and Singtel, *Southeast Asia: An Evolving Cyber Threat Landscape*, March 2015, pp. 3–7. The report does not explicitly attribute the source of attacks to the Chinese government or affiliated APTs, but it does note their belief that "this [intellectual property] often makes its way to Chinese companies."

CHAPTER FIVE

Iran

The Islamic Republic of Iran's cyber operations have come about more recently than either Russia's or China's, beginning around 2004, and are more focused on stifling domestic opposition to the ruling regime and imposing costs on other states for their perceived anti-Iranian activities.[1] Iran's indigenous cyber operations are performed by the Iranian Cyber Army (ICA) and various proxies. Generally, Iranian cyber operations appear to be retaliatory in nature, primarily focused on regional adversaries, and seek to preposition the Islamic Republic in critical infrastructure networks to deter adversaries from intervening in Iran's domestic affairs.

Iran's use of cyber operations evolved as the fears of its own "Velvet Revolution" grew—i.e., domestic unrest and mass mobilization that would overthrow the regime.[2] The regime viewed the internet as a mechanism that would facilitate both domestic and external threats to the regime, a fear validated during Iran's 2009 Green Movement. Iranian cyber operations prior to 2012 employed relatively simple techniques, focusing on things like website defacement.[3] In 2005, the group called the Ashiyane Digital Security Team started a website that offered free hacking tools and tutorials, while also using its members' knowledge and skills to deface websites. While these groups were all sponsored and encouraged by the regime, they were not part of the Iranian military or security apparatus.

The identification of the Stuxnet virus, which targeted Iran's nuclear program in 2010, appears to have spurred Iran to invest in cyber capabilities and to formulate a strategic vision that would enable deterrence against future destructive cyberattacks. It is difficult to determine whether Iran has developed an overarching strategy or doctrine for integrating cyber operations to achieve strategic ends, though it does appear to have the structures in place to do so, such as the Supreme Cyberspace Council,

---

[1] Dorothy Denning, "Following the Developing Iranian Cyberthreat," *Scientific American*, December 12, 2017.

[2] Michael Connell, *Deterring Iran's Use of Offensive Cyber: A Case Study*, Arlington, Va.: CNA Analysis and Solutions, October 2014.

[3] Denning, 2017.

established in 2012.[4] In addition to the ICA, Iran continues to support Ashiyaneh, one of the most prolific hacker groups, which targets sites across Europe, the Middle East, Asia, and the United States; as well as Cyber Hizballah (affiliated with the militant arm of the Islamic Revolutionary Guards Corps [IRGC], the Basij), the Free Cyber Group, the Islamic Cyber Resistance Group, the Izz ad-Din al-Qassam Cyber Forces, Parastoo, and Shabgard.[5]

Iranian national security decisionmaking is difficult for outsiders to discern, given the secrecy of the regime and the existence of structures in which the religious leadership of the country (i.e., the Supreme Leader and the *Majles*) are superior to the President and more "secular" organs of the state.[6] While the Supreme Leader theoretically maintains direct control over all of Iran's armed forces and security services, his decisionmaking style is described as more passive and indirect.[7] This same decisionmaking style may apply to cyber operations as well. Iran's hacktivist groups have therefore operated, at times, independently of the regime. For example, Iranian hacktivists attacked China's Baidu search engine in January 2010, at a time when Iran was trying to build a closer relationship with China.[8]

Although Iran's cyber hacktivist groups vary in degrees of maturity and technical sophistication, they share many basic techniques and tools. According to Hewlett-Packard's Security Research group, Iranian hacktivist groups are heavily influenced by Islamic doctrine, primarily focusing on targets within the United States and in Israel. These groups use a combination of technical and nontechnical tactics to exploit targets, and members are generally well-educated and well-connected.[9] Scholars at the research organization CNA have assessed that Iran has been coordinating with foreign hacktivists with whom Iran shares ideological goals, including Shi'a Islamist hacker groups, the Syrian Electronic Army, and Lebanese Hizballah.[10] The cybersecurity firm Cylance has concluded that the Iranian hacking group Operation Cleaver may share information and conduct joint operations with North Korea.[11] In September 2012, Iran and North Korea signed an agreement for technical cooperation that allows for collaboration in a variety of fields, including IT and security.[12] Other researchers, how-

---

[4] Connell, 2014, p. 4.

[5] Connell, 2014.

[6] See Kevjn Lim, "National Security Decision-Making in Iran," *Comparative Strategy*, Vol. 34, No. 2, 2015.

[7] Connell, 2014, p. 3.

[8] Connell, 2014, p. 12.

[9] Connell, 2014, p. 11.

[10] Connell, 2014.

[11] *#OpCleaver*, Cylance, undated.

[12] *#OpCleaver*, undated.

ever, have sought to downplay the idea that Iran has received significant outside assistance to build its cyber program.[13]

The Shamoon Attacks

In 2012, Iran deployed the Shamoon malware to attack Saudi and Qatari oil and gas companies, demonstrating a major shift in targets, tactics, and level of technical sophistication. Attacks on regional targets, specifically companies in Kuwait, Qatar, Saudi Arabia, and the United Arab Emirates under Operation Cleaver from 2012 through 2014 further refined Iran's more-advanced capabilities that were likely used to attack U.S. and European banks during this time, as well.[14] On August 15, 2012, Iran executed the Shamoon malware on the oil company Saudi ARAMCO, resulting in the destruction of data on three-quarters of the business computers on the company's network. The business networks were segregated from the operational control systems, meaning that the damage did not affect oil production directly. Iran did not claim responsibility for the attack—hackers calling themselves "Cutting Sword of Justice" claimed responsibility—but cybersecurity experts who deployed to Saudi Arabia to assist in the investigation discovered code similar to the Flame virus, which had previously been used in an attack on Iran's Kharg Island oil terminal. The conclusion was that Iran sought to retaliate for that attack.[15]

A January 2017 Shamoon attack on the Saudi petrochemical company Tasnee destroyed hard drives and wiped data, displaying images of Alan Kurdi, a small Syrian child who drowned off the coast of Turkey. This attack further demonstrated Iran's focus on regional—and specifically Saudi Arabian—targets. This attack also occurred during a time when Saudi Arabia was implicated in military operations in Syria that resulted in numerous civilian deaths. The increased sophistication of the Shamoon attacks suggests investment, collaboration, and coordination across multiple Iranian cyber actors as part of a comprehensive operation led by the Iranian regime.[16] This notable increase in technical expertise and evident collaboration among a community of hacking groups suggests that Iran is improving at coordinating its attempts to disrupt adversary organizations and countries, primarily Saudi Arabia.[17]

---

[13] Collin Anderson and Karim Sadjadpour, *Iran's Cyber Threat: Espionage, Sabotage, and Revenge*, Washington, D.C.: Carnegie Endowment for International Peace, 2018, p. 17.

[14] Benjamin Runkle, "America's Arab Allies Should Work Together to Stop Iranian Cyberattacks," *Foreign Policy*, June 6, 2017.

[15] Nicole Perlroth, "In Cyberattack on Saudi Firm, U.S. Sees Iran Firing Back," *New York Times*, October 23, 2012.

[16] Raj Samani and Christiaan Beek, "Shamoon Returns, Bigger and Badder," McAfee, April 25, 2017.

[17] Samani and Beek, 2017.

Tensions between Iran and Saudi Arabia have steadily escalated in recent years, leading some observers to assess that their conflict has been driven online.[18] The mounting tensions between the two nations could explain the more recent August 2017 TRITON cyberattack on Saudi ARAMCO.[19] Although Iran appears to be the most likely perpetrator of this attack, the cybersecurity firm FireEye has concluded that the TRITON intrusion software itself was likely developed by a Russian lab.[20] Unlike past attacks that focused on destroying data or shutting down computer systems, this attack appears to have sought to sabotage the company's operations and trigger an explosion.[21] Specifically, the computer code compromised Schneider Electric's Triconex controllers, which ensure equipment operates within safe parameters. These controllers are reported to be used in roughly 18,000 plants around the world, including in nuclear and water treatment facilities, oil and gas refineries, and chemical plants.[22] A minor mistake in the attacker's computer code prevented an explosion.

The TRITON attack would represent a major escalation in Iran's cyber operations, if indeed Iran was responsible. The potential motives of the attack range from attempts to stunt private sector growth in the Saudi Arabian economy; protesting Saudi Arabia's cut in oil exports, which was itself related to efforts to expand the country's petrochemical and refining industry; to an attempt to complicate Prince Mohammed bin Salman Al-Saud's plan to encourage foreign and private investment to diversify the Saudi economy. These theories seem aimed more at weakening Saudi Arabia economically, rather than coercing it into a specific course of action.[23]

According to Coats, "Iran's leaders are focused on countering what they perceive as a Saudi-led effort to fuel Sunni extremism and terrorism against Iran and Shia communities in the region."[24] Coats also stated that Iran will continue to penetrate U.S. and allied critical infrastructure networks to position itself for future cyberattacks, although Iran's focus remains on its Middle Eastern adversaries.[25] The same dynamic is also evident in Syria, where many Gulf Cooperation Council states support the Syrian rebels against the Islamic State in Iraq and Syria (ISIS), while Iran supports Syrian

---

[18] Nicole Perlroth and Clifford Krauss, "Cyberattack in Saudi Arabia Had a Deadly Goal. Experts Fear Another Try," *New York Times*, March 15, 2018.

[19] Andy Greenberg, "The Iran Nuclear Deal's Unraveling Raises Fears of Cyber Attacks," *Wired*, May 9, 2018.

[20] FireEye, "TRITON Attribution: Russian Government-Owned Lab Most Likely Built Custom Intrusion Tools for TRITON Attackers," October 23, 2018.

[21] Perlroth and Krauss, 2018.

[22] Perlroth and Krauss, 2018.

[23] Perlroth and Krauss, 2018.

[24] Christopher Olsen, "An Introduction to the Implications of Iran's Cyber Capabilities for the U.S.," *Medium*, January 30, 2018.

[25] Courtney Kube, Carol E. Lee, Dan De Luce and Ken Dilanian, "Iran Has Laid Groundwork for Extensive Cyberattacks on US, Say Officials," *NBC News*, July 20, 2018.

President Bashar al-Assad's government. Iran's efforts suggest an orchestrated attempt to challenge its regional adversaries and gain a more prominent place as a regional power.

It appears that Iran is also working to establish both cyber deterrence and a mechanism for retaliation. Through its espionage activities and its infiltration of U.S. critical infrastructure through cyberspace, analysts argue that there is no suggestion of an imminent offensive operation. Instead, Iran may be making preparations that would enable attacks throughout U.S. and EU critical infrastructure networks as a deterrent mechanism, and, if necessary, to establish a retaliation capability.[26]

The timing of Iranian cyber activities has correlated with regional and geostrategic developments—the wars in Yemen and Syria, the identification of Stuxnet that led to the perception of an existential threat to the Iranian regime, or opportunities to promote Iran as a regional great power. In 2015, the timing of the end of attacks on U.S. banks and government agencies coincided with the signing of the Joint Comprehensive Plan of Action (JCPOA).[27] Prior to the deal, cyberattacks between Iran and the United States dominated the news, and Iran systematically carried out repeated attacks against at least 46 financial institutions and companies. While operations targeting the United States diminished, Iran's cyber operations did not cease altogether. Instead, Iran shifted focus back to the Middle East, primarily focusing on the Gulf states and Saudi Arabia.

Iran's use of cyber operations is attended to achieve two main goals: to monitor and control the flow of information domestically, and to retaliate for perceived threats from abroad. It seems less likely, therefore, that its cyber operations are intended to coerce its regional neighbors, though it is possible this will change as Iran's capabilities improve.

---

[26] Kube, Lee, De Luce, and Dilanian, 2018.

[27] Kate Brannen, "Abandoning Iran Nuclear Deal Could Lead to New Wave of Cyber Attacks," *Foreign Policy*, October 2, 2017.

CHAPTER SIX

North Korea

Of any state, North Korea is arguably the most likely to employ cyber operations as part of a coercive strategy. Despite broad consensus about the country's technological backwardness,[1] the North Korean regime has shown remarkable astuteness and dedication by investing in militarily relevant technologies, most prominently in its nuclear and ballistic missile program, but also in recent years in its cyber capabilities.[2]

North Korea has a long history of coercive action, from the shooting down of a U.S. spyplane in the 1960s to the shelling of offshore islands and sinking of a South Korean naval vessel in 2010.[3] For North Korea, these actions have largely paid off, resulting in concessions and economic aid from South Korea and the United States as often as such actions have resulted in more economic sanctions. In this chapter, we examine the 2014 cyber operations against Sony Pictures, and, by extension, the United States.

The North Korean government has not published doctrine or policy specifically addressing its approach to cyber operations; therefore, many of the published reports on how North Korea conceptualizes cyber operations are based on inference or analysis of North Korean behavior.[4] Cybersecurity firms, including FireEye, Kaspersky Labs, and Symantec, attribute at least four APTs to the North Korean government: Lazarus,[5]

---

[1] The North Korean address range for the .kp country domain consists of nine top-level domains and approximately 25 subdomains, according to Recorded Future. Insikt Group, "Shifting Patterns in Internet Use Reveal Adaptable and Innovative North Korean Ruling Elite," Recorded Future, October 25, 2018.

[2] Tom Ball, "Crowdstrike CTO: Theft and Destruction Are 'Just Keystrokes Apart,'" *Computer Business Review*, September 29, 2017.

[3] Sue Mi Terry, "North Korea's Strategic Goals and Policy Towards the United States and South Korea," *International Journal of Korean Studies*, Vol. 17, No. 2, 2013.

[4] See, for example, Emma Chanlett-Avery, Liana W. Rosen, John W. Rollins, and Catherine A. Theohary, *North Korean Cyber Capabilities: In Brief*, Washington, D.C.: Congressional Research Service, August 3, 2017; and Jenny Jun, Scott LaFoy, and Ethan Sohn, *North Korea's Cyber Operations: Strategy and Responses*, Washington, D.C.: Center for Strategic and International Studies, 2015.

[5] Olivia Solon, "WannaCry Ransomware Has Links to North Korea, Cybersecurity Experts Say," *Guardian*, May 15, 2017.

TEMP.Hermit,[6] APT 37 "Reaper,"[7] and APT 38.[8] Their targets include a variety of government and private sector organizations in South Korea and beyond.

Sony Pictures Entertainment

Travis Sharp has argued that the North Korean attack on Sony Pictures Entertainment in November 2014 was a form of cyber coercion aimed at destabilizing Sony's leadership, imposing costs, and seeking to retaliate for perceived insults to the regime with the impending release of a comedy film, the plot of which is focused on an assassination attempt on the North Korean leader.[9] The North Korean regime clearly expressed its opposition to the film's release, but the threats against the company came from other groups, claiming not to work on anyone's behalf but their own. The cyber operations meant to drive the studio to stop the film's release. Sony did, in fact, initially capitulate to this coercion, but reversed the decision after receiving criticism, including from then–President Barack Obama.[10]

The proximate cause of the events was the impending release of the film and North Korea's strong objections to it. As early as June 2014, the North Korean government condemned *The Interview* in a Foreign Ministry statement, and it subsequently sent a letter to the United Nations Secretary General accusing the United States of terrorism and an act of war, demonstrating North Korea's view that Sony's actions were an extension of U.S. policy.[11] After postponing release of the film until December 2014, Sony received demands for money, via email, from a group calling itself God'sApstls, followed by a malware attack that resulted in corruption of the master boot records in numerous computers, rendering them inoperable. A group called Guardians of Peace claimed responsibility for the attack, and began releasing embarrassing emails and yet-to-be released films in the Sony library.[12] This was followed by threats of violence against movie theaters and doxing of Sony executives, through the release of inter-

---

[6]   FireEye, "Attacks Leveraging Adobe Zero-Day (CVE-2018-4878) – Threat Attribution, Attack Scenario and Recommendations," February 2, 2018.

[7]   FireEye, "APT37 (Reaper): The Overlooked North Korean Actor," February 20, 2018.

[8]   Nalani Fraser, Jacqueline O'Leary, Vincent Cannon, and Fred Plan, "APT38: Details on New North Korean Regime-Backed Threat Group," FireEye, October 3, 2018.

[9]   Travis Sharp, "Theorizing Cyber Coercion: The 2014 North Korean Operation Against Sony," *Journal of Strategic Studies*, Vol. 40, No. 7, 2017.

[10]   Greg Jaffe and Steven Mufson, "Obama Criticizes Sony's Decision to Pull 'The Interview'," *Washington Post*, December 19, 2014.

[11]   Patrick Brzeski, "North Korea Files Complaint with United Nations Over *The Interview*," *Hollywood Reporter*, July 11, 2014.

[12]   Jeffrey Roman, "Sony Pictures Cyber-Attack Timeline," BankInfo Security, December 23, 2014.

nal documents that shed them in a bad light. The North Korean government denied responsibility for the attacks and threats but referred to the acts as "righteous deed[s]" and speculated that "supporters and sympathizers" of the North Korean regime were involved.[13] Sony pulled the movie from theaters, but later reversed its decision after President Obama criticized Sony for capitulating to the threats.

Although North Korea denied its involvement in the cyber operations against Sony, North Korea clearly indicated its displeasure with the film for several months prior to the cyber operations. In the summer of 2014, the North Korean Foreign Ministry released a statement that said "[if] the U.S. administration connives at and patronizes the screening of the film, it will invite a strong and merciless countermeasure."[14] Totalitarian regimes often fail to understand how Western countries operate, and conduct their own mirror-imaging. North Korean officials could very well have believed that *The Interview* was part of an official U.S. government propaganda campaign against the regime.

North Korea has a long history of using strong rhetoric, but it has also shown itself willing to use force of various kinds with little compunction, whether through directly attacking military targets, e.g., soldiers along the demilitarized zone or naval vessels, or civilian targets in South Korea. From North Korea's perspective, it is possible that officials felt they had conveyed its message clearly, publicly, and through official channels. The fact that North Korea chose to then follow up on its (failed) coercive rhetoric with cyberattacks through proxies does not draw away from the original intent of the threats. The first phase of coercion, which did not explicitly state the form in which subsequent pain would be inflicted, simply failed to achieve the desired outcome (stopping the film) for more than a few weeks, so the operations had to escalate from threats to action. At that point, the North Koreans were transitioning from the threat of consequences to seeking to impose those consequences; therefore, who delivered those consequences is less important in the moment. At the same time, U.S. officials noted that they were not clear on how the threat against the movie theaters playing the film was intended to be carried out, which did not detract from the officials treating it as a serious threat.[15]

Whether the North Koreans truly believed that the use of proxy fronts (likely the Reconnaissance General Bureau and the Korean People's Army) would obfuscate the origins of the threats is an interesting question, but it is currently unanswerable. If the North Koreans indeed sought to hide their direct involvement, then it is questionable that it would contribute to the credibility of future coercive threats. That said, the North Koreans have routinely denied responsibility for physical attacks—e.g., the sinking of the *Cheonan* naval vessel in 2010—when no other credible perpetrators

---

[13] "North Korea: Supporters Hacked Sony Over Comedy 'The Interview,'" *Reuters*, December 7, 2014.

[14] Brzeski, 2014.

[15] Sharp, 2017.

present themselves.[16] It is conceivable that the North Koreans deny their involvement as a *pro forma* matter as opposed to seeking to avoid blame. This denial also plays to their domestic audience, where the regime has to portray itself constantly as the victim, rather than the aggressor. Sharp concludes that, while not necessarily achieving all of its aims, the Sony cyberattack shows a successful use of cyber operations, coupling cyber exploitation (the stealing of data) with offensive cyber to disable computers to coerce Sony's leadership.

North Korea's cyber capabilities are not exclusively retaliatory, nor does the regime likely see them as a replacement for other forms of coercion.[17] The country's ongoing nuclear and missile programs are likely still seen as guarantors of regime survival. But cyber operations provide a flexible new tool to achieve a variety of ends—theft to improve the regime's finances, espionage, and threats and infliction of pain and damage on its adversaries. The recent cyber operations also establish a track record of use that could play a role in future coercive scenarios.

---

[16] Terry, 2013.

[17] Jun, LaFoy, and Sohn, 2015.

CHAPTER SEVEN

Conclusion and Next Steps

As this report has demonstrated, the circumstances surrounding the use of cyber operations to coerce are often ambiguous, contrary to what published theory would lead one to believe. Thus far, however, the track record of states using cyber operations to coerce others and achieve the desired change in behavior is poor. This raises the question: Should we care that states may be using cyber operations to coerce if the consequences of these operations are minor? The recent history is not an indication that cyber operations will not become more destructive in the future; therefore, the threat of cyber operations could lead to more successful coercion.

This is an area that merits more study to identify the conditions in which states can use cyber operations to coerce more successfully, and what states can do to anticipate, deter, or mitigate such circumstances. Rather than wait for the day when one state can hold another hostage under the threat of cyber-induced destruction, now is the time to grapple with this problem. We conclude with some ideas on where to take this research next to best inform policymakers.

States are not clearly signaling either threats or expected behavior, let alone the means they might use to coerce others. More work is needed to understand conflict dynamics where cyber coercion functions as a tool that states will seek to apply. It may be difficult to discern whether cyber operations directed against a country are intended to coerce or have some other motivation. As noted in the China cases, the evidence is not strong that cyber espionage was intended to have a coercive element, but there is the possibility.

We recommend two approaches to further our understanding. The first is to hold a series of tabletop exercises with regional and functional experts to explore scenarios where coercion might occur. The coercing state in this game would be given a set of tools, including cyber operations, which the team can choose to employ or not. The central idea is to use the game to explore conflict dynamics—not coercion specifically—to see whether and why the coercing state chooses to use cyber operations, and whether the other teams recognize the activity as intending to coerce. The second method is to use game theory to explore the dynamics in which a state benefits from employing cyber operations to coerce. Game theory provides a rigorous theoretical basis for exploring these issues. The two approaches in combination can provide complementary insights.

The early signs of potential cyber coercion can look similar to other more- or less-malicious cyberactivity: scanning of networks; phishing emails; and perhaps social engineering, developed from scraping of websites for information.[1] This indicates that more work is needed to create indicators to provide warning of emerging cyber coercion. Such indicators will need to build from a combination of technical and nontechnical inputs to ensure that the geopolitical context is correlated with technical indicators of possible compromise.

Finally, a state needs to think through how it will respond to attempted cyber coercion well in advance of an actual case emerging. It is often too late to take decisive action, except in response, when in the midst of a crisis. As a state explores the circumstances in which cyber coercion might arise, and has developed indicators to support a warning network, it should also examine how it can use these insights to inform strategies for deterring, responding to, and mitigating the effects of cyber coercion. There is already a strong base of literature exploring how to apply deterrence frameworks to address cyberthreats.[2]

Recognizing and countering cyber coercion is not an easy task, as this report has demonstrated. Not all of the cases examined in this report are clear acts of cyber coercion, which highlights the complexity of determining the motivations behind malicious cyberactivity. Embedding the technical analysis of cyber operations in the broader understanding of state-to-state (and nonstate) actors' relations can provide the context to understand when and how cyber coercion may occur. Establishing a framework for countering cyber coercion in the future requires understanding the conflict dynamics that make cyber coercion more likely to emerge; developing the means to detect early signs of cyber coercion; and crafting deterrence and resiliency strategies. This framework will give the United States and its partners the tools to respond successfully to cyber coercion as it emerges.

---

[1] Website scraping is not always malicious and cannot always be discerned, except by inference such as repeated requests from the same Internet Protocol address.

[2] These include Joseph S. Nye, Jr., "Deterrence and Dissuasion in Cyberspace," *International Security*, Vol. 41, No. 3, Winter 2016/2017 ; Scott Jasper, "Deterring Malicious Behavior in Cyberspace," *Strategic Studies Quarterly*, Vol. 9, No. 1, Spring 2015; and Martin Libicki, *Cyber Deterrence and Cyberwar*, Santa Monica, Calif.: RAND Corporation, MG-877-AF, 2009.

Bibliography

Ambinder, Marc, "Did America's Cyber Attack on Iran Make Us More Vulnerable?" *The Atlantic*, June 5, 2012. As of January 4, 2019:
https://www.theatlantic.com/national/archive/2012/06/
did-americas-cyber-attack-on-iran-make-us-more-vulnerable/258120/

Anderson, Collin, and Karim Sadjadpour, *Iran's Cyber Threat: Espionage, Sabotage, and Revenge*, Washington, D.C.: Carnegie Endowment for International Peace, 2018.

Applebaum, Anne, "Why Does Putin Want to Control Ukraine? Ask Stalin," *Washington Post*, October 20, 2017. As of January 6, 2018:
https://www.washingtonpost.com/outlook/why-does-putin-want-control-ukraine-ask-stalin/2017/10/20/800a7afe-b427-11e7-a908-a3470754bbb9_story.html?utm_term=.9fb81

Assante, Michael J., "Confirmation of a Coordinated Attack on the Ukrainian Power Grid," SANS Industrial Control Systems, January 9, 2016. As of January 5, 2018:
https://ics.sans.org/blog/2016/01/09/confirmation-of-a-coordinated-attack-on-the-ukrainian-power-grid

Bajrović, Reuf, Vesko Garčević, and Richard Kraemer, *Hanging by a Thread: Russia's Strategy of Destabilization in Montenegro*, Philadelphia: Foreign Policy Research Institute, June 2018. As of November 19, 2018:
https://www.fpri.org/wp-content/uploads/2018/07/kraemer-rfp5.pdf

Ball, Tom, "Crowdstrike CTO: Theft and Destruction Are 'Just Keystrokes Apart,'" *Computer Business Review*, September 29, 2017. As of December 29, 2017:
https://www.cbronline.com/news/cybersecurity/
crowdstrike-cto-theft-destruction-just-keystrokes-apart/

Bing, Chris, "APT28 Targeted Montenegro's Government Before It Joined NATO, Researchers Say," *CyberScoop*, June 6, 2017. As of November 19, 2018:
https://www.cyberscoop.com/apt28-targeted-montenegros-government-joined-nato-researchers-say/

Bodine-Baron, Elizabeth, Todd C. Helmus, Andrew Radin, and Elina Treyger, *Countering Russian Social Media Influence*, Santa Monica, Calif.: RAND Corporation, RR-2740-RC, 2018. As of November 26, 2018:
https://www.rand.org/pubs/research_reports/RR2740.html

Borghard, Erica D., and Shawn W. Lonergan, "The Logic of Coercion in Cyberspace," *Security Studies*, Vol. 26, No. 3, 2017, pp. 452–481.

Branigan, Tania, "South Korea on Alert for Cyber Attacks After Major Network Goes Down," *Guardian*, November 20, 2013. As of January 6, 2018:
https://www.theguardian.com/world/2013/mar/20/south-korea-under-cyber-attack

Brannen, Kate, "Abandoning Iran Nuclear Deal Could Lead to New Wave of Cyber Attacks," *Foreign Policy*, October 2, 2017. As of January 4, 2019:
https://foreignpolicy.com/2017/10/02/abandoning-iranian-nuclear-deal-could-lead-to-new-wave-of-cyberattacks/

Brzeski, Patrick, "North Korea Files Complaint with United Nations Over *The Interview*," *Hollywood Reporter*, July 11, 2014. As of December 29, 2017:
https://www.hollywoodreporter.com/news/north-korea-files-complaint-united-717943

Cao Zhengrong, Wu Renbo, and Sun Jianjun, eds., *Informationized Joint Operations* [信息化联合作战], Beijing: People's Liberation Army Press, 2006.

Chanlett-Avery, Emma, Liana W. Rosen, John W. Rollins, and Catherine A. Theohary, *North Korean Cyber Capabilities: In Brief*, Washington, D.C.: Congressional Research Service, August 3, 2017.

Chase, Michael S., and Arthur Chan, *China's Evolving Approach to "Integrated Strategic Deterrence,"* Santa Monica, Calif.: RAND Corporation, RR-1366-TI, 2016. As of December 1, 2018:
https://www.rand.org/pubs/research_reports/RR1366.html

Cheng, Dean, "Chinese Views on Deterrence," *Joint Force Quarterly*, No. 60, 2011, pp. 92–94.

Cheng, Jonathan, and Josh Chin, "China Hacked South Korea Over Missile Defense, U.S. Firm Says," *Wall Street Journal*, April 21, 2017. As of April 20, 2018:
https://www.wsj.com/articles/chinas-secret-weapon-in-south-korea-missile-fight-hackers-1492766403

Coats, Dan, "Statement for the Record: Worldwide Threat Assessment of the Intelligence Community," testimony before the Senate Select Committee on Intelligence, Washington, D.C.: Director of National Intelligence, May 11, 2017.

Connell, Michael, *Deterring Iran's Use of Offensive Cyber: A Case Study*, Arlington, Va.: CNA Analysis and Solutions, October 2014.

Connell, Michael, and Sarah Vogler, *Russia's Approach to Cyber Warfare*, Arlington, Va.: CNA Analysis and Solutions, September 2016.

Costello, John, and Joe McReynolds, *China's Strategic Support Force: A Force for a New Era*, Washington, D.C.: National Defense University Press, October 2018.

Council on Foreign Relations, "Cyber Operations Tracker," webpage, undated. As of March 1, 2019:
https://www.cfr.org/interactive/cyber-operations

Cylance, *#OpCleaver*, undated.

Davis, Joshua, "Hackers Take Down the Most Wired Country in Europe," *Wired*, August 21, 2008. As of May 1, 2018:
https://www.wired.com/2007/08/ff-estonia/.

Defense Science Board, *Task Force Report: Resilient Military Systems and the Advanced Cyber Threat*, Washington, D.C.: U.S. Department of Defense, January 2013.

———, *Task Force on Cyber Deterrence*, Washington, D.C.: U.S. Department of Defense, February 2017.

Denning, Dorothy, "Following the Developing Iranian Cyberthreat," *Scientific American*, December 12, 2017. As of July 12, 2018:
https://www.scientificamerican.com/article/following-the-developing-iranian-cyberthreat

Elkind, Peter, "Inside the Hack of the Century," *Fortune*, June 25, 2015. As of January 4, 2018:
http://fortune.com/sony-hack-part-1/

Finnemore, Martha, "Cybersecurity and the Concept of Cyber Norms," Washington, D.C.: Carnegie Endowment for International Peace, November 30, 2017. As of December 2, 2017:
http://carnegieendowment.org/2017/11/30/cybersecurity-and-concept-of-norms-pub-74870

FireEye, "Advanced Persistent Threat Groups: Who's Who of Cyber Threat Actors," webpage, undated. As of November 12, 2018:
https://www.fireeye.com/current-threats/apt-groups.html

———, "Attacks Leveraging Adobe Zero-Day (CVE-2018-4878) – Threat Attribution, Attack Scenario and Recommendations," February 2, 2018. As of December 20, 2018:
https://www.fireeye.com/blog/threat-research/2018/02/attacks-leveraging-adobe-zero-day.html

———, "APT37 (Reaper): The Overlooked North Korean Actor," February 20, 2018. As of December 20, 2018:
https://www.fireeye.com/blog/threat-research/2018/02/apt37-overlooked-north-korean-actor.html

———, "TRITON Attribution: Russian Government-Owned Lab Most Likely Built Custom Intrusion Tools for TRITON Attackers," October 23, 2018. As of November 27, 2018:
https://www.fireeye.com/blog/threat-research/2018/10/triton-attribution-russian-government-owned-lab-most-likely-built-tools.html?wpisrc=nl_cybersecurity202&wpmm=1

FireEye iSight Intelligence, *Russia's APT 28 Strategically Evolves Its Cyber Operations*, January 11, 2017.

FireEye and Singtel, *Southeast Asia: An Evolving Cyber Threat Landscape*, March 2015. As of March 1, 2019:
https://www.fireeye.com/content/dam/fireeye-www/current-threats/pdfs/rpt-southeast-asia-threat-landscape.pdf

Fifield, Anna, "South Korea, U.S. to Start Talks on Anti-Missile System," *Washington Post*, February 7, 2016. As of April 19, 2018:
https://www.washingtonpost.com/world/south-korea-united-states-to-start-talks-on-thaad-anti-missile-system/2016/02/07/1eaf2df8-9dc4-45e3-8ff1-d76a25673dbc_story.html?noredirect=on&utm_term=.d32ee78e01b3

"Foreign Ministry Sees Hike in Cyberattack Attempts from China This Year," *Yonhap News Agency*, September 10, 2017. As of April 19, 2018:
http://english.yonhapnews.co.kr/national/2017/09/10/0301000000AEN20170910001300315.html

Fraser, Nalani, Jacqueline O'Leary, Vincent Cannon, and Fred Plan, "APT38: Details on New North Korean Regime-Backed Threat Group," FireEye, October 3, 2018. As of March 1, 2019:
https://www.fireeye.com/blog/threat-research/2018/10/apt38-details-on-new-north-korean-regime-backed-threat-group.html

Gartzke, Erik, "The Myth of Cyberwar: Bringing War in Cyberspace Back Down to Earth," *International Security*, Vol. 38, No. 2, 2013, pp. 41–73.

Glaser, Bonnie S., Daniel G. Sofio, and David A. Parker, "The Good, the THAAD, and the Ugly," *Foreign Affairs*, February 15, 2017. As of April 19, 2018:
https://www.foreignaffairs.com/articles/united-states/2017-02-15/good-thaad-and-ugly

Greenberg, Andy, "How an Entire Nation Became Russia's Test Lab for Cyberwar," *Wired*, June 20, 2017. As of July 6, 2017:
https://www.wired.com/story/russian-hackers-attack-ukraine

———, "The Iran Nuclear Deal's Unraveling Raises Fears of Cyber Attacks," *Wired*, May 9, 2018. As of December 1, 2018:
https://www.wired.com/story/iran-nuclear-deal-cyberattacks/

Groll, Elias, "Feds Quietly Reveal Chinese State-Backed Hacking Operations," *Foreign Policy*, November 30, 2017. As of November 14, 2018:
https://foreignpolicy.com/2017/11/30/feds-quietly-reveal-chinese-state-backed-hacking-operation/

Hollis, David, "Cyberwar Case Study: Georgia 2008," *Small Wars Journal*, 2011.

Hultquist, John, "Sandworm Team and the Ukrainian Power Authority Attacks," FireEye, January 7, 2016. As of January 5, 2018:
https://www.fireeye.com/blog/threat-research/2016/01/ukraine-and-sandworm-team.html

Indictment, *United States v. Internet Research Agency*, Case 1:18-cr-00032-DLF (D.D.C. February 16, 2018). As of December 1, 2018:
https://www.justice.gov/file/1035477/download

Insikt Group, "Recorded Future Research Concludes Chinese Ministry of State Security Behind APT3," Recorded Future, May 17, 2017. As of November 14, 2018:
https://www.recordedfuture.com/chinese-mss-behind-apt3/

———, "Shifting Patterns in Internet Use Reveal Adaptable and Innovative North Korean Ruling Elite," Recorded Future, October 25, 2018. As of October 30, 2018:
https://www.recordedfuture.com/north-korea-internet-usage/

Jaffe, Greg, and Steven Mufson, "Obama Criticizes Sony's Decision to Pull 'The Interview'," *Washington Post*, December 19, 2014. As of April 12, 2019:
https://www.washingtonpost.com/politics/obama-criticizes-sonys-decision-to-pull-the-interview/2014/12/19/77d1ce9a-87ad-11e4-b9b7-b8632ae73d25_story.html?utm_term=.a58348a40fc3

Jasper, Scott, "Deterring Malicious Behavior in Cyberspace," *Strategic Studies Quarterly*, Vol. 9, No. 1, Spring 2015, pp. 60–85.

Jensen, Benjamin M., Brandon Valeriano, and Ryan C. Maness, "Cyber Compellence: Applying Coercion in the Information Age," undated. As of November 26, 2018:
https://www.brandonvaleriano.com/uploads/8/1/7/3/81735138/cyber_victory.pdf

Jervis, Robert, *Perception and Misperception in International Politics*, Princeton, N.J.: Princeton University Press, 1976.

Johnson, David E., Karl P. Mueller, and William H. Taft, *Conventional Coercion Across the Spectrum of Operations: The Utility of U.S. Military Forces in the Emerging Security Environment*, Santa Monica, Calif.: RAND Corporation, MR-1494-A, 2003. As of December 23, 2017:
https://www.rand.org/pubs/monograph_reports/MR1494.html

Jun, Jenny, Scott LaFoy, and Ethan Sohn, *North Korea's Cyber Operations: Strategy and Responses*, Washington, D.C.: Center for Strategic and International Studies, 2015.

Kamphausen, Roy, David Lai, and Andrew Scobell, eds., *Beyond the Strait: PLA Missions Other than Taiwan*, Carlisle, Penn.: Strategic Studies Institute, 2009

Keane, Jonathan, "Hackers Tried to Disrupt the Parliamentary Elections in Montenegro," *Digital Trends*, October 17, 2016. As of March 1, 2019:
http://www.businessinsider.com/hackers-tried-to-disrupt-the-parliamentary-elections-in-montenegro-2016-10

Komnenic, Peter, "Thousands Protest Against Montenegro's Government," *Reuters*, October 18, 2015. As of November 19, 2018:
https://www.reuters.com/article/us-montenegro-protests-idUSKCN0SC0SR20151018

Kube, Courtney, Carol E. Lee, Dan De Luce and Ken Dilanian, "Iran Has Laid Groundwork for Extensive Cyberattacks on US, Say Officials" *NBC News*, July 20, 2018. As of January 4, 2019:
https://www.nbcnews.com/news/us-news/
iran-has-laid-groundwork-extensive-cyberattacks-u-s-say-officials-n893081

Libicki, Martin C., *Cyber Deterrence and Cyberwar*, Santa Monica, Calif.: RAND Corporation, MG-877-AF, 2009. As of March 1, 2019:
https://www.rand.org/pubs/monographs/MG877.html

Lim, Kevjn, "National Security Decision-Making in Iran," *Comparative Strategy*, Vol. 34, No. 2, 2015, pp. 149–168.

Mahnken, Thomas G., Ross Babbage, and Toshi Yoshihara, *Countering Comprehensive Coercion: Competitive Strategies Against Authoritarian Political Warfare*, Washington, D.C.: Center for Strategic and Budgetary Assessments, May 30, 2018.

Martina, Michael, and Greg Torode, "Chinese Wary Over U.S. THAAD Missile System Because Capabilities Unknown, Experts Say," *Reuters*, April 3, 2017. As of April 20, 2018:
https://www.reuters.com/article/us-usa-china-missiles-idUSKBN1752PP

McCauley, Martin, *The Soviet Union 1917-1991*, London, UK: Longman, 1993.

McReynolds, Joe, "China's Evolving Perspectives on Network Warfare: Lessons from the Science of Military Strategy," *China Brief*, Vol. 15, No. 8, April 16, 2015.

McWhorter, Dan, "Mandiant Exposes APT1–One of China's Cyber Espionage Units & Releases 3,000 Indicators," FireEye, February 19, 2013. As of November 13, 2018:
https://www.fireeye.com/blog/threat-research/2013/02/mandiant-exposes-apt1-chinas-cyber-espionage-units.html?utm_source=rss

Meick, Ethan, and Nargiza Salidjanova, *China's Response to U.S.-South Korean Missile Defense System Deployment and its Implications*, U.S.-China Economic and Security Review Commission, July 26, 2017. As of April 19, 2018:
https://www.uscc.gov/sites/default/files/Research/Report_China%27s%20Response%20to%20THAAD%20Deployment%20and%20its%20Implications.pdf

Minárik, Tomáš, Raik Jakschis, and Lauri Lindström, eds., *2018 10th International Conference on Cyber Conflict, CyConX: Maximising Effects*, Tallinn, Estonia: NATO CCD COE Publications, 2018.

Ministry of Defense of the Russian Federation, *Conceptual Views on the Activities of the Armed Forces of the Russian Federation in the Information Space* [Концептуальные взгляды на деятельность Вооруженных Сил Российской Федерации в информационном пространстве], 2011. As of May 1, 2018:
http://ens.mil.ru/science/publications/more.htm?id=10845074@cmsArticle

Ministry of Foreign Affairs of the Russian Federation, "Comment by the Information and Press Department on Invitation for Montenegro to Start Talks on Joining NATO," December 2, 2015. As of November 19, 2018:
http://www.mid.ru/cn/foreign_policy/news/-/asset_publisher/cKNonkJE02Bw/content/id/1963259

———, "Comment by Foreign Ministry Spokesperson Maria Zakharova on New Threats of Sanctions from the United States," December 28, 2016. As of January 6, 2018:
http://www.mid.ru/en/foreign_policy/news/-/asset_publisher/cKNonkJE02Bw/content/id/2581641.

"Montenegro: Caught in the Midst of the East-West Conflict," *Deutsche Welle*, October 23, 2015. As of November 19, 2018:
https://www.dw.com/en/montenegro-caught-in-the-midst-of-the-east-west-conflict/a-18802732

Mulvenon, James, "PLA Computer Network Operations: Scenarios, Doctrine, Organizations, and Capability," in Roy Kamphausen, David Lai, and Andrew Scobell, eds., *Beyond the Strait: PLA Missions Other than Taiwan*, Carlisle, Penn.: Strategic Studies Institute, 2009.

"NATO Invitation to Montenegro Prompts Russia Warning," *BBC News*, December 2, 2015.

Nye, Joseph S., Jr., "Nuclear Lessons for Cyber Security?" *Strategic Studies Quarterly*, Vol. 5, No. 4, Winter 2011, pp. 18–38.

———, "Deterrence and Dissuasion in Cyberspace," *International Security*, Vol. 41, No. 3, Winter 2016/17, pp. 44–71.

North Atlantic Treaty Organization, "Partnership for Peace Programme," webpage, 2017. As of April 30, 1019:
https://www.nato.int/cps/en/natohq/topics_50349.htm

"North Korea: Supporters Hacked Sony Over Comedy 'The Interview,'" *Reuters*, December 7, 2014. As of March 12, 2018:
http://www.newsweek.com/north-korea-supporters-hacked-sony-over-comedy-interview-289899

Olsen, Christopher, "An Introduction to the Implications of Iran's Cyber Capabilities for the U.S.," *Medium*, January 30, 2018. As of January 4, 2019:
https://medium.com/@chrisolsen97/us-implications-of-irans-cyber-capabilities-c4f88d3e2745

Park Byong-su, "South Korea's 'Three No's' Announcement Key to Restoring Relations with China," *Hankyoreh*, November 2, 2017. As of April 19, 2018:
http://english.hani.co.kr/arti/english_edition/e_international/817213.html

Peng Guangqian and Yao Youzhi, The Science of Military Strategy [战略学], Beijing, China: Military Science Press, 2005.

Perlroth, Nicole, "In Cyberattack on Saudi Firm, U.S. Sees Iran Firing Back," *New York Times*, October 23, 2012. As of January 30, 2019:
https://www.nytimes.com/2012/10/24/business/global/cyberattack-on-saudi-oil-firm-disquiets-us.html

Perlroth, Nicole, and Clifford Krauss, "Cyberattack in Saudi Arabia Had a Deadly Goal. Experts Fear Another Try," *New York Times*, March 15, 2018. As of November 18, 2018:
https://www.nytimes.com/2018/03/15/technology/saudi-arabia-hacks-cyberattacks.html

Perper, Rosie, "North Korea May Be Behind a Massive Cyber Attack on a South Korean Bitcoin Exchange that Caused It to Collapse," *Business Insider*, December 21, 2017. As of January 6, 2018:
http://www.businessinsider.com/north-korea-south-korea-bitcoin-heist-2017-12

President of the Russian Federation, "Decree of the President of the Russian Federation from 31 December 2015, No. 683, *About the National Security Strategy of the Russian Federation* [Указ Президента Российской Федерации от 31.12.2015 г. № 683, О Стратегии национальной безопасности Российской Федерации]," December 31, 2015.

———, "Decree of the President of the Russian Federation from 5 December 2016, No. 646, *About the Approval of the Doctrine of Information Security of the Russian Federation* [Указ Президента Российской Федерации от 05.12.2016 г., № 646, Об утверждении Доктрины информационной безопасности Российской Федерации]," December 5, 2016.

President's Commission on Critical Infrastructure Protection, *Critical Foundations: Protecting America's Infrastructures*, Washington, D.C, October 13, 1997.

Rogers, Michael S., *Statement of Admiral Michael S. Rogers, Commander, United States Cyber Command, Before the Senate Committee on Armed Services*, May 9, 2017. As of December 1, 2018:
https://www.armed-services.senate.gov/imo/media/doc/Rogers_05-09-17.pdf

Roman, Jeffrey, "Sony Pictures Cyber-Attack Timeline," BankInfo Security, December 23, 2014. As of December 30, 2017:
https://www.bankinfosecurity.com/sony-pictures-cyber-attack-timeline-a-7710

Runkle, Benjamin, "America's Arab Allies Should Work Together to Stop Iranian Cyberattacks," *Foreign Policy*, June 6, 2017. As of January 4, 2019:
https://foreignpolicy.com/2017/06/06/americas-arab-allies-should-work-together-to-stop-iranian-cyberattacks/

"S. Korea, China to Be Affected by THAAD Fall Out: Think Tank," *Yonhap News Agency*, May 3, 2017. As of April 19, 2018:
http://english.yonhapnews.co.kr/business/2017/05/03/0501000000AEN20170503002700320.html

Samani, Raj and Christiaan Beek, "Shamoon Returns, Bigger and Badder," McAfee, April 25, 2017. As of November 18, 2018:
https://securingtomorrow.mcafee.com/business/shamoon-returns-bigger-badder/

Sanger, David E., and William J. Broad, "Trump Inherits a Secret Cyberwar Against North Korean Missiles," *New York Times*, March 5, 2017.

Schelling, Thomas C., *Arms and Influence*, New Haven, Conn.: Yale University Press, 1966.

Sharp, Travis, "Theorizing Cyber Coercion: The 2014 North Korean Operation Against Sony," *Journal of Strategic Studies*, Vol. 40, No. 7, 2017, pp. 898–926.

Shou Xiaosong, ed., *The Science of Military Strategy* [战略学], Beijing, China: Military Science Press, 2013.

Solon, Olivia, "WannaCry Ransomware Has Links to North Korea, Cybersecurity Experts Say," *Guardian*, May 15, 2017. As of December 20, 2018:
https://www.theguardian.com/technology/2017/may/15/wannacry-ransomware-north-korea-lazarus-group

Son, Hyo-Ju, "Chinese Hackers Attack S. Korean Military Websites," *Dong-a Ilbo*, March 21, 2017. As of April 19, 2018:
http://english.donga.com/Home/3/all/26/876623/1

Stefan-Gady, Franz, "China to Embrace New Active Defense Strategy," *Diplomat*, May 26, 2015. As of December 29, 2017:
https://thediplomat.com/2015/05/china-to-embrace-new-active-defense-strategy/

Swaine, Michael D., "Chinese Views on South Korea's Deployment of THAAD," *China Leadership Monitor*, No. 52, Winter 2017. As of April 19, 2018:
https://carnegieendowment.org/files/CLM52MS.pdf

Terry, Sue Mi, "North Korea's Strategic Goals and Policy Towards the United States and South Korea," *International Journal of Korean Studies*, Vol. 17, No. 2, 2013, pp. 63–92.

ThreatConnect, "Belling the Bear," updated October 7, 2016. As of November 14, 2018:
https://threatconnect.com/blog/russia-hacks-bellingcat-mh17-investigation/#.V-wnrubaeEU.twitter

Treisman, Daniel, "Why Putin Took Crimea: The Gambler in the Kremlin," *Foreign Affairs*, April 18, 2016. As of January 6, 2018:
https://www.foreignaffairs.com/articles/ukraine/2016-04-18/why-putin-took-crimea

Tucker, Patrick, "Russia Will Build Its Own Internet Directory, Citing US Information Warfare," *DefenseOne*, November 28, 2017. As of November 29, 2017:
http://www.defenseone.com/technology/2017/11/russia-will-build-its-own-internet-directory-citing-us-information-warfare/142822/

U.S. Department of Defense, *DOD Dictionary of Military and Associated Terms*, undated. As of January 1, 2019:
https://www.jcs.mil/Portals/36/Documents/Doctrine/pubs/dictionary.pdf

———, *The Department of Defense Cyber Strategy*, Washington, D.C., 2015.

———, *Summary: Department of Defense Cyber Strategy 2018*, Washington, D.C., 2018. As of November 15, 2018:
https://media.defense.gov/2018/Sep/18/2002041658/-1/-1/1/CYBER_STRATEGY_SUMMARY_FINAL.PDF

Valeriano, Brandon, and Ryan C. Maness, "The Dynamics of Cyber Conflict Between Rival Antagonists, 2001–11," *Journal of Peace Research*, Vol. 51, No. 3, 2014.

Verizon, *2018 Data Breach Investigations Report: Tales of Dirty Deeds and Unscrupulous Activities*, 2018. As of November 19, 2018:
https://enterprise.verizon.com/resources/reports/dbir/

Wang Houqing and Zhang Xingye, *The Science of Military Campaigns* [战役学], Beijing, China: National Defense University Press, 2000.

Wang Zhengde, *Information Confrontation Theory* [信息对抗论], Military Science Publishing House, 2007.

The White House, *National Cyber Strategy of the United States of America*, September 2018.

Whyte, Christopher, "Ending Cyber Coercion: Computer Network Attack, Exploitation and the Case of North Korea," *Comparative Strategy*, Vol. 35, No. 2, 2016, pp. 93–102.

Ye Zheng, "A Discussion of the Innate Characteristics, the Composition of Forces, and the Included Forms [论网络空间战略博戏的本质特征，力量构成与内容形势]," *China Information Security* [中国信息安全], August 2014.

Yeo Jun-suk, "China Launches Cyberattacks Against South Korea in Protest of THAAD: Former US Navy Commander," *Korea Herald*, April 27, 2017. As of April 19, 2018:
http://www.koreaherald.com/view.php?ud=20170427000945

Yuan Yi, "A Rough Analysis of the Characteristics, Categories, and Utility of Deterrence in the Cyberspace [浅析网络空间威慑的特征，类型，和运用要点]," *China Information Security*, No. 11, 2015.

Yuan Wenxian, ed., *Lectures on Joint Campaign Information Operations* [联合战役信息作战教程], Beijing, China: Military Science Press, 2009.

Zivanovic, Maja, "Russia's Fancy Bear Hacks its Way Into Montenegro," *BalkanInsight*, March 5, 2018. As of November 18, 2018:
https://www.balkaninsight.com/en/article/
russia-s-fancy-bear-hacks-its-way-into-montenegro-03-01-2018